DEMCO

i

<u>Dedication</u>

I dedicate this book to my Mom who made me practice spelling and English, even when I didn't want to do it, and was a role model for reading – the key to my continuing education in life. Thanks Mom!

I would also like to dedicate this book to my coach from seventh grade through high school – Mr. Joel Baba. His most famous saying, "It's not what you do, but how you do it that counts." Advice as specific and valuable then as it is now. Thanks, Coach!

Finally, I would also like to dedicate this book to my buddies at Brothers Pizza who let me take over a booth in the back when I was writing my very first book and supplying a slice of pizza and a drink when this poor writer was short on funds. Brother's Pizza still has the best pizza and cheese steaks in the world (in Langhorne, PA). Thanks, Sal, Pat, John, and Big Sal! Check out John making me a mushroom pizza!

Back Handsprings
The Secret Techniques

Rik Feeney

Richardson Publishing
Altamonte Springs, Florida

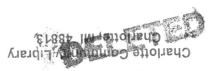

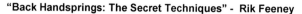

"Back Handsprings: The Secret Techniques" - Rik Feeney

Richardson Publishing, Inc.
PO Box 162115
Altamonte Springs, FL 32716
www.GymnasticsTrainingTips.com

ISBN: 978-0-9637991-9-7   **LCCN: 2006904545**

DISCLAIMER

This book is written and intended for use as a guide only. The publisher and author are not engaged in the profession of rendering any form of legal, technical, or medical advice. If for any reason legal, technical or medical advice is necessary, you should seek out qualified professionals.

> Any activity, especially one with a high degree of motion, rotation, and height, many times in an inverted (upside-down) position, carries with it a greater potential for injury than normal daily activity. Landing on the head or neck could cause serious and irreparable harm with the potential for fatal consequences to the individual. For this reason, it is advised / demanded that you seek initial training from a Safety Certified gymnastics or cheer coach before using this material for any other purpose.

The purpose of this book is to educate and acquaint individuals with basic safety concepts and training methods used in acrobatics, gymnastics, and tumbling. Every effort has been made to provide complete and accurate information on this subject. Readers of this book are strongly advised to obtain guidance and instruction from USAG Safety Certified Coaches or Instructors or Coaches with Risk Management Certifications through the USAG (USA Gymnastics) as well as Certification in GYMCERT'S Level's 1 to 3, and knowledge through the "Safety Basics for Gymnastics Instructors" book. Available online at **www.GymnasticsTrainingTips.com**

The author and Richardson Publishing shall have neither liability nor responsibility to any person or entity with respect to any injury, loss, or damage caused or alleged to be caused directly or indirectly by the information contained in this book.

> Note: Illustrations included with this text are approximations only. Adjustments to equipment, gymnast, and training conditions may be required. In addition, all skills should be spotted by a competent and qualified gymnastics, cheerleading, or tumbling coach until the athlete is competent and confident to do the skill on her own. Whether an illustration depicts a spotter or not, use one for all athletes training these drills.

Contents

Basic Safety Guidelines for Tumblers

1. Tumbling is a fun activity, however, lack of focus during technical training, the performance of the skill, or in the workout area in general can lead to the potential of catastrophic injury. **Pay attention to your coach and the activity at hand.**

2. Use of any type of gymnastics, cheerleading, or tumbling equipment should only occur in the presence of qualified supervision.

3. Use appropriate progression techniques with regard to your physical conditioning, your knowledge of the timing, sequence, and specific attributes of the skill being performed, and the equipment necessary to each progression level.

4. In all training situations, proper matting, appropriate to the skill and progression level of the athlete should be used. Consult your coach.

5. Safe landing skills should be practiced for all tumbling skills and specifically for surfaces that are outside normal workout conditions.

6. **Always ask for a spot!** If you are ever in doubt about the safe performance of a tumbling skill, because of fear, lack of training, unusual conditions, or just a gut feeling – ask for a spot.

7. Responsibility for the performance of tumbling skills, and the potential for injury, outside the normal workout area and the guidelines listed here rests completely with the performer and the supervisor (parent, coach, director, etc.) of the activity.

8. In all instances, focus on preparing a safe environment for the performance of tumbling skills, which may include crowd control, hydration of athletes, shelter from the elements, and continuous checks of equipment to make sure it is in safe and acceptable working condition.

9. Prepare an "**Emergency Action Plan**" to implement in case of accident or injury.

10. **Always focus on Safety!**

Acknowledgments

This book has been a dream/goal of mine for some time and would not have been possible without help from Buffy Purdom, Bill Purdom, Jade Holzer, Sandy Holzer, and Tasha Muizulis. Thank you all.

Thanks to all my former employers, co-workers, gymnasts, and cheerleaders I coached. The information in this book comes from the years I spent working with each of you.

Thanks to Rita Brown a mentor and collaborator in other writing projects.

Special thanks to Frank Mannina of FM Print Management in Altamonte Springs, Florida for helping with the production and development of the final product.

Special thanks to the following companies for providing products, resources, equipment, and advice.

Varsity Spirit Fashions   Cheerleader & Danz Team
www.varsity.com   www.nationalspirit.com

800.533.8022   800.527.4366

continued next page...

www.alphafactor.com
800.825.7428

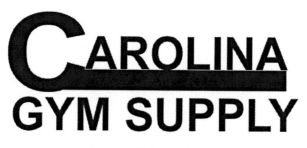

www.carolinagym.com
info@carolinagym.com

Carolina Gym Supply
575 Dimmocks Mill Road
Hillsborough, NC 27278

877-496-7883 – Toll free.
919-732-1510 – Fax

Foreword

Any activity in life from taking a bath, playing basketball, even walking home after school carries varying degrees of risk for potential injury. An elbow in the face during a jump shot, a twisted ankle stepping off the curb, or a slip and fall getting out of the bathtub may cause serious injury. There is also the potential for significant injury when learning gymnastic, acrobatic, and tumbling skills.

The key to success for any athlete[1] is patience, a desire to learn, and guidance from a qualified coach. Your desire to learn is obvious by the fact you are reading this book to learn and understand back handspring technique. **Note:** The skills presented are based on one "average" (in size, shape, and fitness level) athlete, which may be illustrated for some drills and techniques[2]. While the techniques presented may work adequately for this fictitious athlete, they may not work as well for the slightly overweight and less physically fit athlete. Some of you may need some preparatory work with strength training and nutrition.[3]

Responsibility for the use and/or adaptation of these techniques is the sole responsibility of the individual using them. The information contained in this guide

---

[1] Because a back handspring is a popular tumbling skill for gymnasts, cheerleaders, dancers, martial artists, or anyone wanting to learn how to tumble, I will use the generic term "athlete" or "tumbler" throughout the text. In addition, demographics suggest more individuals of the female persuasion will read this book, so the pronoun of choice throughout the text will be "she" or "her."
[2] Illustrations are designed as visual cues but may not in all instances be completely accurate. If in doubt about anything in this book, check with a qualified gymnastics coach for clarification.
[3] Weight loss techniques should only be practiced under the specific guidance of your family doctor or any specialist your family doctor recommends.

provides a base level of knowledge about gymnastics, acrobatic, and tumbling skills and training techniques for the back handspring in particular. Contact qualified coaches from a local gymnastics or cheer program to guide you in developing effective techniques for a back handspring, as well as spotting skills and training methods specific to your needs.

Note to Mom & Dad

Throughout this book I will be talking primarily to the athlete, however, coaches and parents may listen in for information and ideas. Parent's, please defer to your coach's instructions regarding specific advice on your daughter's back handspring training.

This book is a guide, not a license to lecture the coach!

When in doubt about a back handspring technique, always check with your local professional gymnastics and/or cheer coach for guidance.

* * * * * * *

Athletes, get ready to start your engines!

You probably receive offers in the mail every day for "get back handsprings quick" schemes. You may be disturbed at dinner time by phone calls from telemarketer's trying to sell you the "latest" drill that will not only teach you the back handspring in ten minutes but make you popular in school and the person most likely to be discovered for a part in the next reality television show.

And, you know, for a very few that dream may come true but I wouldn't bet a month's supply of hair products on it.

My all encompassing goal for this book is that you learn how to do a back handspring **SAFELY** while having **FUN** learning. That means there are no shortcuts. Strength and flexibility will be the primary ingredient for your success in this endeavor, however, a safe environment (matting, spotters, etc.), an understanding of technique, and, of course, motivation are also important.

What I am trying to say is it will take focused effort on your part. There is no magic wand or special pixie dust to endow you with this skill. It has been said that "repetition is the mother of skill," and I believe that to be true, when you also add "feedback" to refine the skill, and "variety" to keep the whole process interesting and motivating.

It takes as long as it takes

I have not had the pleasure of meeting you in person so I can't make a determination of your current level of fitness, your past background in acrobatics, gymnastics, or tumbling, or your current level of desire. I assume you have a high level of desire since you have purchased this book – thanks, by the way.

So, how long will it take to learn a back handspring?

It takes as long as it takes and I do suggest that you take your time. You will refine the back handspring through hundreds of repetitions of drills and techniques. Long after you get your back handspring, you will review these skills time and again to continually refine your skill.

Throughout the whole process of learning a back handspring, I ask/desire/command you to focus on Safety (always), then fun, but certainly and without a doubt, I ask that you hold this one thought in your mind on every attempt: *"I will do my best!"*

Athletes, raise your right hand[4]

Repeat after me.

*"I do solemnly swear on my best pair of shoes and tightest jeans that I will read this book cover to cover and study every page **BEFORE** attempting any of the techniques, drills, or the back handspring itself. So help me, Bela!"*[5]

---

[4] See page 119 in the appendix for a copy of the Safety Oath which should be prominently displayed in your home workout area.
[5] That is a reference to the famous gymnastics coach Bela Karolyi who not only develops champions, but gives great bear hugs and is useful for carrying injured athletes. Heck, I wouldn't mind if he carried me around for a bit.

Introduction

Welcome to *"Back Handsprings: The Secret Techniques."* By the fact that you are reading this book, I can already tell that you are a determined and intelligent athlete. Your curiosity will be rewarded with several drills and skills that will make learning a back handspring a safe, fun, and meaningful goal.

First, let me tell you that I have been a gymnast, coach, gymnastics club owner and author for over thirty years, so I do have quite a bit of experience teaching back handsprings – literally hundreds of thousands (maybe millions) of them to gymnasts in recreational classes and team gymnasts, many of whom also learned how to do them on a balance beam, which is only four-inches wide and four feet off the ground! I have also worked as a tumbling coach with cheerleaders at the high school and college level.

Let me be clear that this is a book for anyone who wants to learn how to do a back handspring whether you are a gymnast, a cheerleader, a dancer, a martial artist, or a stunt person – in short, anyone[6] who would like to add a back

---

[6] This includes instructors, coaches, physical educators, and activity sponsors or supervisors.

handspring to his or her personal list of extraordinary abilities.[7]

A back handspring is not a difficult skill, but it will require time and physical effort to make it a goal which is achieved in a safe and sane manner.

Before we continue, I have a question for you.

What is your experience with tumbling skills?

The reason I ask is you do need a solid grounding in the basic tumbling skills (I.E. forward roll, backward roll, handstand, and cartwheel,[8]) before moving on to a back handspring.

You can acquire these skills through physical education classes at school or enrolling in tumbling classes at a private gym, dance, or martial arts center. It won't take long and the training in handstands and cartwheels will be especially important in learning a back handspring and other lead-up skills.

Okay, let's break your goal (a back handspring) down to the four most important areas you need to focus on:

1. Appropriate Conditioning That means strength & flexibility and skill specific exercises. (See basic exercises on pages xvii and xviii.)

2. Proper training. What you learn from this book combined with guidance from an experienced coach in a tumbling program near you.

---

[7] This book is also a great reference for parents who want to help; however, I strongly advise that you learn how to spot from a qualified gymnastics coach in a safely matted facility.

[8] The handstand and cartwheel are necessary building blocks of the back handspring and round off back handspring.

3. The **proper environment** for learning the skill.[9] I know that cheerleaders, martial artists, dancers, and stunt persons will perform these skills in a variety of settings; however, when first learning a back handspring, I think it is safest to learn in a properly matted and supervised setting.

4. Overwhelming desire to learn the skill. You really have to want this skill to get it.[10] After all, how many "normal" people do you know who can flip over backwards then snap down and land standing on their feet? You will be one of a small, but elite community of athletes that can demonstrate a body awareness that enables you to do such a skill.

Going for it!

Overwhelming desire will also help you overcome **FEAR**, which stands for *False Experience Appearing Real*. I have yet to see any athlete get hurt attempting a back handspring who was going for the skill 100%. Fear is normal. I was scared the first time I did a back handspring. Heck, I was still scared on my five hundredth attempt, but I went for it!

Going for the back handspring (when properly trained and prepared) 100% is the key to success. When your coach says it is time; give it everything you have and you will be pleasantly surprised.

Blah, blah, blah...

I know, you just want me to get on with it so you can get to working on your back handspring, however, I do need

---

9 See www.carolinagym.com for planning your gym/home workout area.
10 By "get it" I do not mean "just get by." I mean you have an awesome "stand out from the crowd" back handspring.

to touch on a few more things before we get to the training.

Safety Issues

For years, I advised my athletes not to practice back handsprings and other tumbling skills at home. Yet, when I review my childhood, I have to confess that I practiced back handsprings at home, jumped on the neighbor's trampoline, and did all the things kids are still doing today. I know that parents spot kids at home, and that many youngsters tumble in the grass. Heck, the jungle gym, and swing set at school are dangerous; even the family bathtub is cause for more injuries than this one tumbling skill.

The conclusion I came to is that kids will work on back handsprings at home no matter what I (or their coaches) say, so why not help them to be safe and train correctly? That is my goal with this book; to provide each reader the information on how to do a back handspring safely and successfully in conjunction with a professional gymnastics or cheer coach.

Beyond this introduction, training for the back handspring begins quickly with special skills and drills. I ask that athletes, parents, coaches, and instructors be sure to read the material placed in the Appendix of this book. The material is no less important because of its position in the book design.

Again, thank you for reading this book. I hope that you learn your back handspring in a safe and enjoyable manner.

Basic Strength Exercises

Basic push ups:

Reverse Leg Lift

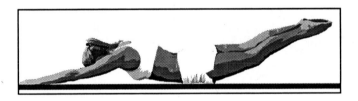

Arch Up

Tuck Sit Ups

Carpet cleaners

Mushies

(Mushies are stretch or tuck jumps on a port-a-pit)

1 – Secret Techniques

The Back Handspring is for tumbling enthusiasts what the Holy Grail was for religious zealots; something to be obtained, coveted, and revered at any cost. While a back handspring truly is a worthy goal, like the Holy Grail, it is not an object that can be found, held, or bought at a price other than the hard work of the athlete. Along with the round off, a back handspring is one of the key or core elements used in all levels of acrobatics / gymnastics / tumbling.

Secret 1: Knowledge

As you already know from reading the back cover of this book, getting hold of the appropriate knowledge is a major key for your success. You will find several techniques and drills in this book to help you in learning a back handspring.

Let me be the first to say that the techniques presented are "a" way, not "the" only way to train back handsprings. Always seek the advice of a professional, qualified gymnastics or cheerleading coach when in doubt about what technique is best for you.

Secret 2: Magic doesn't work!

> *"Eye of newt;*
> *Old bat's wing;*
> *Give a lazy athlete;*
> *A back handspring!"*

Wouldn't it be fabulous if, just by uttering a spell or magical incantation, you could get a back handspring with no effort at all!

Guess what? There is a secret magical technique that can do just that! The magical technique I am talking about is called Conditioning.

I hear you groaning in frustration! Cut it out; do you want to hurt my feelings?

Seriously, the quickest and safest way to get a competent back handspring is to be in good physical condition.

Tumbling skills require more abdominal and / or upper arm strength than the average person needs in daily activities. Without this strength, what usually happens when performing a back handspring is the athlete's arms bend or her legs bend or come apart so she can make it past the handstand position without landing on her head.

Pretend you are an athlete that weighs 100 pounds. When you jump slightly up and backward to do a back handspring you don't just land with just 100 pounds of weight on your hands, you have to add in the power from the force of your jump too.

The power you put into the jump could multiply the force you have to control, which could be two to three times your body weight!

Normally, you are only passing through the handstand position for a very brief moment before punching out of your shoulders, and with proper muscular tension, you can control this position safely. But, what if your jump is not powerful enough, or on takeoff you jump too high and your body goes straight up and straight back down again?

That could result in the now famous, yet painful, nose pose on the floor.

The three biggest areas of concern regarding Strength (one aspect of conditioning) are:

    1. **Quadriceps strength** (upper thigh) for power in jumping back to the handstand position (see "mushies" p. xviii);

    2. **Upper arm and shoulder strength** to support the body in the handstand position (see pp. xvii & xviii); and,

    3. **Abdominal** (stomach) **and hip flexor strength** to pull your lower body through the handstand position, and then over into a snap down to finish the back handspring (see p. xviii).

Flexibility (the other aspect of conditioning) also plays an important role in getting a back handspring. If you have not stretched your abdominal muscles appropriately, you will experience a new sensation in pain as you strain stomach muscles for the first time as you actively do a back handspring. (A bridge is a good exercise to stretch abdominals and shoulders.)

Good shoulder flexibility allows you to keep your arms in a straight line (next to your ears) in relation to the rest of your body. The importance here is in maintaining straight body lines.[11] For now, just remember that the least number of lines you make with your body parts – the better the technique.

---

[11] More about the importance of body lines in chapter 9.

So, if your shoulders and upper back lack flexibility, your arms will tend to be in front of your ears creating two distinct body lines. (See illustration at right)

If you jump backward into a back handspring with two body lines; one from your hands to your shoulders and continuing into space; and, the other line going from your head to your toes, you are sure to land in a position that will be very difficult to control unless you have the shoulder strength of the Incredible Hulk™.

Your goal

To be as strong as you can throughout as wide a range of motion as possible in all muscle groups of the body.[12] The purpose of this chapter has been to impress upon you the need for strength and flexibility and the effect it will have on your getting a quality back handspring that is not only technically correct, but will lead to higher level tumbling skills, which will make you stand out from the crowd – just like magic!

---

[12] For more information on strength and flexibility, please see the Special Reports online at **www.GymnasticsTrainingTips.com**. **Special Note**: Before beginning any new workout program, you should have a physical examination by a medical doctor. In addition, it is both prudent and advisable to schedule a private lesson with a qualified tumbling / gymnastics coach who can evaluate your strength and flexibility and make recommendations specific to your needs.

Secret 3: Basics, Basics, Basics

While this book primarily focuses on one specific skill – the back handspring – it is important that you have competent/proficient/quality basic tumbling skills:

- the forward roll;
- the backward roll;
- the cartwheel: and,
- the handstand.

Arguably, these four fundamental skills combined with appropriate conditioning are the foundation or building blocks from which all other acrobatic / gymnastic / tumbling skills arise.[13] Enroll in a tumbling program sponsored by a local gymnastics facility, cheer program, YMCA, Parks and Recreations Department, local dance academy or martial arts program and take classes to develop your basic skills. It certainly won't hurt to do a refresher course as well.

Yes, I know I already covered much of this in the first few pages, but as I have stated before, Repetition is the mother of skill (and knowledge). And, if you recognized that this is a rewording of earlier material then you have proof that repetition works! You will find that I repeat many safety and technical ideas throughout the book to make sure these ideas are totally ingrained into your thinking process.

---

[13] Some would argue that the element of "swing" is also a fundamental skill. Swing takes place when the body rotates around an outside object or one body part rotates about another body part.

Special Note: Good Technique vs. Bad Technique

Sometimes a particular skill or drill I have you practice contains a fragment of a technique that is especially helpful in teaching the back handspring. Learning a back walkover to get a kinesthetic sense (a feeling) of going backwards through a handstand position is helpful in training a back handspring, however, the overall skill may be detrimental to the long-term training of a back handspring.

Why?

A back walkover is considered a flexibility move. Standing in place with one leg forward, you use the flexibility in your shoulders and back to slowly reach backward into a handstand and push off with your support leg and kick over with the other leg to a stand.

A back handspring is supposed to be more dynamic, a move designed to cover distance and develop power as a setup for the next skill, which, in many instances, is some form of somersault.

Initially, I may ask you to use a back bend to kick over, a back limber, or a back walkover to develop your awareness for backward oriented skills, but I will soon modify those techniques for the more appropriate power related drills once you have demonstrated a level of confidence and competence in performance of these skill fragments.

*   *   *   *   *

2 – The Handstand[14]
(Secret 4)

While I have already mentioned the handstand when talking about basics, I have not given it the acclaim it deserves. To do that, I have devoted this whole chapter to the handstand.

I have heard it said that in many ways the sport of gymnastics is a "moving handstand," intermingled with additional unique body shapes but always passing through / punching out of / returning to / and holding and highlighting this body position.

What I most often see practiced in gym classes is not a handstand, but what I like to call a "balanced arch."

Imagine a young child playing with building blocks attempting to create a single-column tower. The first few blocks on the bottom of the tower are "square" or in alignment with each other, but as the tower grows taller, one block is placed a little too far to the left, so the next block must counterbalance a little too far to the right. The tower continues to grow maintaining a precarious balance until ultimately it is too unstable and falls.

Many gymnasts kick up to a handstand and assume a precarious balance position by letting their stomachs sag on one side and their backs arch on the other side and like the tower of blocks eventually become too unstable and fall out of the handstand position.

---

[14] See "Secret of Gymnastics Success: The Handstand" at www.GymnasticsTrainingTips.com .

"What does this have to do with a back handspring?" The answer: Everything

Advanced level skills are developed from the perfection and stylization of basic skills.

Would you want to live in a high rise building if you knew the builders used weak materials in the foundation; the structure that holds the whole building together?

I wouldn't.

So why would you build a back handspring with a poor foundation in basic skills? The answer is you don't. The key to a solid foundation in the handstand is the next secret.

Secret 5: Core Stability

The "core" I am talking about is the torso of your body (I.E. everything but your arms, legs, and head). The definition of stability is when you can hold your torso in a slightly hollowed position and maintain this position for the duration of the skill, drill, or technique.

Conditioning for the Handstand[15]

I could now bore you in a vain attempt to make you think I am a genius by talking about **muscles that help with core stability.** Muscles that also help to control balance like: the abdominals, erector spinae, serratus anterior, quadratus lumborum, pectoralis and hip flexors (peripheral support) and possibly even the intercostals,

---

[15] See Basic Strength Exercises on pages xvii and xviii.

but do you really think you or I will ever make it to the "lightning round" on Jeopardy?[16]

Instead, I will suggest you do lots of bent knee or tuck sit ups to **strengthen your abdominals** allowing you to keep the stomach sucked in and tight (see p. xviii).

For your **back muscles**, I suggest **arch ups & reverse leg lifts** on the floor for building up strength (see p. xvii).

And, to complete a basic torso conditioning program, get someone to hold your feet while you are on your side on the floor doing **side sit ups**.

<u>**Warning:**</u> **Make sure you are doing each exercise properly by consulting with a qualified gymnastics / cheer coach.**

<u>**Note:**</u> **Before doing any type of exercise, check with your doctor to be sure you are in good physical condition and capable of performing these exercises safely.**

---

[16] See http://www.innerbody.com/text/musc19-new.html for detailed pictures of the muscular system.

Body A-line-ment

When standing in stretch position[17] with your **shoulders down** but with your arms close to your ears and pointing straight up you are essentially creating one straight line with your body.

When kicking up to the handstand, you want to maintain a straight line from your palms to the tips of your toes. The only break in your body line will occur when you lift one leg to step forward into the skill.

Most athletes will kick up to a handstand from a **lunge position** (front leg bent), although the degree to which you bend your leg and how much force you use to push off the ground may vary with each attempt at the skill causing differences in your control of the position.

Ultimately, kicking up into a handstand from a straight front leg is the ideal although **you must have excellent flexibility** in your hamstrings and lower back muscles to perform the kick up from this position without straining muscles or tendons.

---

[17] See Appendix A: Basic Body Positions for Gymnastics.

Hand Position

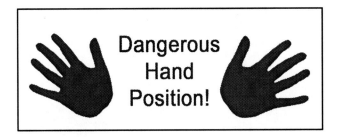

In both the handstand and the back handspring, it is very important that you **position your hands correctly** to prevent injury to the wrists, elbows, and arms. If your **hands** are **turned out,** you can cause the elbows to lock which **could lead to hyperextension injuries, dislocations, or worse.** One safe way to place your hands on the floor during a handstand or back handspring is:

1. Put your arms straight out in front of you, shoulder-width apart, with your palms facing toward the floor with all your fingers pointing forward.

2. With your palms still facing toward the floor stick your thumbs out to the side and slowly bring your arms together until the tips of your thumbs are touching each other.

3. Now, extend both wrists upward so your fingers point toward the ceiling.

4. With thumbs touching and fingers pointing toward the ceiling, rotate your hands until the index fingers on both hands are almost touching. Done correctly, you will notice that you have created a somewhat triangular space between your thumbs and index fingers (see Figure 1 on page 30).

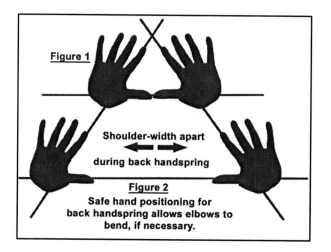

5. Keeping your hands in this slightly turned in position, separate your arms again until they are shoulder-width apart (see Figure 2). This is an appropriate hand placement on the floor for handstands and back handsprings – of course, your arms will be up next to your ears and not in front of your body when performing the skill.

Balance

Pretend you are inside a box, with both arms up in the air next to your ears. The front and sides of the box are only one to two inches from your body. When you kick up into a handstand, that's about all the room you have to move without losing your balance and falling out of the handstand position.

(The athlete at the right is slightly relaxed in the lower back and letting her heels drift and could be more hollow in the chest.)

Note: With regard to balance, as your hands contact the floor, spread your fingers apart to cover a broader surface area of support. Your hands will make several small adjustments to help you maintain control of your balance in the handstand position. If you start to fall forward, you can press out of your fingers more, or if you start to fall back, you can press out of the heels of your hands. Balance, especially in the beginning, may be a dynamic process.

Handstand Drills:

- ## Handstands with Body Shaping

Start your handstand training with the help of your coach. As stated earlier, your focus should be on core body tightness, which you might well believe you have accomplished until your coach starts tucking your seat under, makes you suck in your stomach, has you pull your toes toward the ceiling, and generally manipulates your body into the proper position. The idea is to develop a "kinesthetic memory" or an idea of how the handstand should feel to you when being performed correctly.

- ## Handstand against the wall

Once you have a good sense of how a proper handstand should feel, you can then begin to practice the handstand by yourself up against a wall that is padded or has an 8-inch landing cushion propped up and secured.

Start from a lunge position, keeping a straight line from your fingertips to the end of the toes on your kick up leg, and place your hands on the floor approximately 6-inches from the wall/mat while pushing out of the bottom leg and kicking up with the other leg. See if you can close both legs together before they actually reach the handstand position.

Obviously, you may overbalance and have to use your hands and abdominal muscles to pull back off the wall/mat to recover the handstand position. You only need to practice a handstand about 5,212 times until you get it perfect.

- **Beyond Handstand**

One of the keys to being a top athlete is the ability to recover from mistakes and make it all look like it was planned in the first place. Most athletes practicing a handstand tend to hold back when practicing without a spotter or the support of a wall/mat. The fact is many times you are going to kick up harder than necessary and instead of bailing out, you should first practice a recovery drill called the "beyond handstand."

Kick up to a handstand against the wall/mat as described in the previous drill, except this time place your hands about 12-18 inches away from the wall / mat. This should put you into an overbalanced, arched handstand position.

Now, without using your feet to push off the wall/mat, press out of your arms and shoulders and begin pulling your legs back to the handstand position using your abdominal muscles and hip flexors until you are in a controlled handstand position.

Secret 6: Safe Recovery Drills
(from the Handstand Position)

Earlier, I made a comment about "bailing out." Bailing out can either mean you gave up on the attempt or you needed to regain control without getting hurt. Since I know you are a determined athlete, I will assume any time you bail out it is to regain control. However, some ways of bailing out may be better than others.

For instance, I am not a fan of novice tumblers attempting to forward roll out of a handstand position when they lose their balance. *The head and neck should always be protected,* yet if a novice tumbler rolls out of a handstand; the first thing she does is bend her arms and hopefully tuck her head under in time. If she starts to roll but her legs don't continue over, but actually step back down in the opposite direction, she could end up compressing her neck with potentially negative consequences.

I also do not care for stepping down to the side like a cartwheel or twisting the body round off style to turn out of the handstand as a bail out plan. I believe there is a potential for injury to the wrist and elbow of the arm you are twisting toward and, quite simply, I think it is practicing a bad habit to allow this type of "recovery."[18]

Basic Recovery Drills from a Handstand

- ### Drill: Step back down through an arabesque.

Sorry, no fireworks or spectacular techniques, simply step back down to the floor. When your first foot touches the floor, immediately lift your head and chest while holding your back leg at a 45° angle to step out through an arabesque position.

---

[18] Remember, this is my book and **my opinions**, not necessarily facts. I don't ask that you blindly agree with me, but please give it some consideration.

• <u>Drill: Handstand to Bridge-Over Recovery</u>

The first few times, the best way to practice this recovery drill is with a spotter and/or performed over a foam barrel. Simply kick up to the handstand position a little harder than normal, and then use your abdominal muscles to lower your legs slowly forward into a bridge position. You can also press your shoulders backward over your hands to act as a counterbalance for your legs.

Sometimes, you may find yourself falling over lickety-split, with little time to think about what to do, so just bend your legs so you land feet first and help keep yourself from landing flat on your back or compressing your head and neck.

<u>Secret 7: Repetition</u>

Now, get to work! You have at least 5,212 handstands to practice before you get it perfect, and remember: (say after me…)

"Repetition is the mother of skill;
Feedback is the father of refinement;
Variety is the crazy uncle that keeps it interesting; but,
Motivation is an inner drive fueled by intense Desire; and,
Success is my reward for determination and effort;
however, throughout it all,
Preparation and Supervision are the keys to my Safety"

- Rik Feeney

(I think that should be a T-shirt.)

Always Focus on Safety!

3 – Awareness Drills
(Secret 8)

Awareness Drills for Back Handsprings

One potential problem in teaching any type of gymnastics, acrobatic, or tumbling skill is providing a frame of reference from which to begin the training. Since you spend most of your life with your head above your feet and very little time upside down, I will provide you with drills that will not only acquaint you with the upside-down position, but help you to feel comfortable in it.

The first drill to build awareness you already worked in the last chapter – the handstand. Following are some additional drills to build your awareness and control when upside-down.

- ## Drill: A bridge.[19]

    Purpose: To develop a directional awareness (where am I?) in your body in a semi-inverted (mostly upside-down) position. In addition, the quality of your bridge indicates how good your flexibility is in your shoulder, abdominal, quadriceps, and hip flexor muscles.

    Directions: Start by lying down on a mat. While lying flat on your back bend both knees, pulling your feet up close to your hips, with the soles of your feet flat on the floor.

---

[19] A bridge may also be called a back bend or limber over position.

Next, bend both arms and place the palms of your hands on the mat next to your ears with your fingers pointing toward your shoulders.

Once you have positioned both legs and arms appropriately, push down against the mat with both arms and legs, lifting your hips and stomach up toward the ceiling.

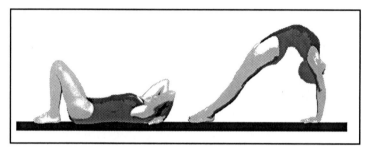

Your arms should be shoulder-width apart and covering your ears.

Most athletes want to look at their hands on the floor, but this is not ideal and could lead to poor technique later during a back handspring, so you will start this skill by learning to keep your head in a neutral position - between your arms.

Ideally, you should have enough shoulder flexibility to straighten your arms and by pushing backward out of your legs, you should be able to position your shoulders directly over your hands.

Warning: Be careful moving into this position. You might find that your shoulder and abdominal muscles are very tight or you have no flexibility in your upper back. Lack of flexibility in the upper back could be the result of a limited range of motion between the vertebrae (those bumps[20] down the middle of your back).

Forcing yourself to go beyond the normal range of motion by bouncing, having a partner pull you, or putting yourself on a torture rack will do nothing more than cause you injury, which in turn could cause your muscles to become even tighter.

Steady, controlled stretching over the next few weeks is the best way to improve your flexibility.

Important Note: By the way, you will note throughout this book that I use several different models, both gymnasts and cheerleaders, and while they have done an excellent job, I don't want you to attempt to specifically duplicate what you see. Some pictures highlight one aspect of a skill I want you to visualize but not necessarily all aspects. I am not that good a photographer and the ladies get tired doing the same skill repeatedly. So, use the illustrations as a guideline only, and refer to your gymnastics / cheer coach for specifics regarding your attempts at the skill.

The next drill is...

- **Drill: The Rocking Bridge**
  (back and forth, side to side)

Purpose: To learn how to shift your weight from your shoulders to your feet and vice versa.

---

[20] Those "bumps" are a part of the vertebrae in your back called the spinous process. In some people, the overlapping part of the vertebrae, or spinous process, has little room between itself and the next spinous process, causing a distinct lack of flexibility that may not be solved by any amount of stretching.

Directions: Push up into a bridge position from a lying position on the floor, then push out of your shoulders until your body weight is distributed with more emphasis on your legs. Next, push out of your legs until your body weight is primarily situated over your shoulders and hands. Slowly, move your body weight back and forth between your shoulders and your legs until you can comfortably rock back and forth.

Once you can successfully rock back and forth, practice rocking side to side, so your weight shifts primarily to the left, and then back to your right.

- **Drill: Hands off – feet off.**

Purpose: To advance your understanding of the process of shifting your weight.

Directions: In this drill, you will rock back and forth like the above drill but you will attempt to lift your feet off the ground when you shift your weight to your shoulders, and lift your hands off the ground when you shift your weight to your feet.

The ultimate result of this drill will be the ability, one day, to stand up on your feet as though finishing a limber over, or to pull through your stomach and hip flexors with enough strength and fluid motion from rocking onto your hands to pull your legs up into a handstand position.

Don't get carried away and attempt a rocker drill to stand or handstand right now unless you are an accomplished gymnast, abnormally flexible, or your coach says it is okay. The key is to learn a back handspring safely, not get injured doing drills.

- ## Drill: (Bridge) Right side off; left side off.

Purpose: This is an advanced drill for learning to shift your weight side to side.

Directions: Similar to the hands off – feet off drill, you will rock your body by shifting your weight side to side this time rather than shoulders to feet and as you do so lift the arm and leg on one side off the ground briefly and then alternate to the other side by shifting your weight back again.

- ## Drill: (Bridge) Alternating arms & legs

Purpose: To develop bilateral symmetry[21] in nerve impulses and brain function, or in simpler terms; build your body's ability to function on the right and left sides with equal talent.

Directions: Push up into a bridge position and practice lifting the right arm and left leg up into the air for three seconds. Put them back down and then lift the left arm and right leg into the air.

---

[21] To speed recovery from injury, many times physical therapists will work the uninjured side of the body. Somehow there is a transference not only between complementary body parts, which helps speed the healing of the injured part, but also in the case of the brain; a build up of the bridge between hemispheres, called the corpus callosum, which develops more integrated right and left brain activity.

Okay, those were the introductory awareness drills for learning a back handspring. Now, you are going to move on to some more difficult awareness drills.

At this point, you may be saying to yourself, *"But, Coach Rik why do we need to do all these drills?"*

I suppose you could simplify the back handspring technique to a very basic format:

From a stand, with both arms above your head, jump backwards to a handstand position, and then follow through to a snap down and land in a standing position.

(Don't do it! This is a mental exercise.)

Simple, right?

Maybe, for that one in a million athlete who is not only naturally talented but is in perfect shape physically and also missing the fear gene from her DNA that the rest of us were handed at birth – sometimes called common sense.

The teaching of a back handspring can be relatively straightforward, however, going for it by yourself for the first time is best accomplished as a step by step process where you demonstrate success and develop your confidence and competence in a series of safe skill progressions. Always remember that Safety is your focus on every skill attempt.

Always Focus on Safety!

4 - Locomotor Bridge Drills
(Secret 9)

- ### Drill: Walk in a bridge across the floor

Purpose: to coordinate the hands and feet in movement in a forward and backward direction while upside-down.

Directions: Starting near the edge of the floor exercise mat or one end of your panel mat, push up into a bridge position. While in the bridge position, move the right hand and the left foot six-inches in the direction of travel across the mat. Repeat the process with the left hand and the right foot. Continue alternating hands and feet in this manner until you reach the other side of the mat (leading with the hands first, and then coming back leading with the feet first across the floor).

Safety Note: Finish the bridge walk well before you run out of matting so you don't lower from the bridge position and bang your head on the floor.

- ### Drill: Walk in a bridge sideways
(across the floor on both right and left sides)

Purpose: To get a feel for lateral or sideways motion while almost upside-down.

Directions: On a mat or floor exercise carpet, push up into a bridge position, and then move both your left hand and left leg six-inches away from your body. Next, move your right hand and right leg six-inches closer to your body. Repeat this process until you have traveled across the mat or Floor exercise carpet.

- **Drill: Walk in a circle**
  (clockwise & counter clockwise)

Purpose: When you are upside-down your sense of direction goes all out of whack. To help you understand where you are you will do this drill in both directions, clockwise and counter-clockwise.

Directions: Push up into a bridge position on a mat. The easiest way to begin is by bringing the right hand next to the left, then slide the left hand a small distance away, then bring the right hand in close again. If you do the same thing with your feet while moving your hands, your body will begin to turn. After mastering a turn in one direction, practice turning in the other direction.

This can be a frustrating drill in the beginning, when you find your hands constantly trying to go in the wrong direction. Be patient and work at it.

Lower Back Relief

After doing several bridges your lower back and shoulders may become sore. Upon finishing the drills, lie down on your back and do the following exercises:

1. Keeping the right leg straight and flat against the floor, pull your left knee up to your chest and hold this position for 30 – 60 seconds.

2. Switch and tuck your right leg while straightening the left leg and again hold for 30 – 60 seconds.

3. Grab hold of both knees in a loose tuck and rock back and forth for 30 – 60 seconds.

4. You can also sit in a pike position and bend your left knee so you can place your left foot on the ground on the outside of your right knee. Now take your right arm and place the back of your elbow against the outside of your left knee and begin to push your left knee as far to the right as you can. Done correctly, you will feel a stretch on the outside of your left hip and your lower back. Switch arms and legs and do the stretch to the other side also.

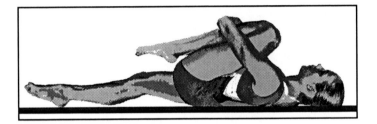

Always Focus on Safety!

5 – Bridge: Floor Drills
(Secret 10)

- **Drill: Bridge kickover from panelite mats.**
  - **From two mats**
  - **From one mat**
  - **From the floor**

Purpose: To help you do a bridge kick over with no spotter.

Directions: On the floor exercise mat, fold up one panelite mat (or two panelite mats and place one on top of the other). Lie down so your hips are up against the mats, with your feet on top of the mats and your hands on the floor next to your ears. Push up into a bridge position with your feet up on the mats and your hands on the floor ex mat. Next, push out of your legs until your shoulders are over your hands, then kick over to a stand one leg at a time.

Once you have mastered this drill with two mats you can take one mat away and practice kicking over with just the one mat. Again, upon mastery of this skill you can flip the mat halfway open and practice kicking over until you can finally do a kick over from the floor.

- **Drill: Bridge to limber over from mats**
  - **From two mats**
  - **From one mat**
  - **From the floor**

Purpose: To learn how to shift the lower body weight to the shoulders and pull through hips flexors, abdominal muscles and shoulder muscles to pull the lower body up into a handstand and over to finish in a push up position[22].

Directions: On the floor exercise mat, fold up two panelite mats and place one on top of the other. Lie down so your hips are up against the mats, with your feet on top of the mats and your hands on the floor next to your ears. Push up into a bridge position, and then push out of your

---

[22] You will finish in a push up position because piking down (sometimes tucking) tends to become a habit. This "not-so-good" habit places your body in a position where the block and repulsion through the arms, shoulders, and chest, necessary for advanced tumbling, becomes more difficult.

legs until your shoulders are over your hands, then pull through the abdominal and hip flexor muscles while continuing to push out of your shoulders to bring your legs up into a handstand position. Follow through to a landing in a push up position.

Follow a similar technique with one mat, and then finally, begin by pushing up to a bridge from lying on the floor and limbering over to a push up position.

- ### Drill: Reach Back to Bridge on Wedge Mat

NOTE: Practice this drill after practicing the "Wall Drills" in the next chapter.

    Purpose: To learn how to reach back into a bridge safely from a standing stretch position.

Ask for a spot when you need help!

    Directions: Take a wedge mat (incline/decline mat), sometimes called the "Cheese" mat because of its shape and place it with the higher end of the wedge against the wall. Use one or two spotters on either side of you to support your hips. Start in stretch position and carefully reach through your fingertips back and down to the wedge mat until you are in the bridge position.

Important Technique Notes – Back Limber

If you felt a bounce in your shoulders upon contact with the mat, then you did not truly reach to the mat, you actually fell to the mat. This is a lack of control that must be corrected before it continues into a bad habit.

Causes and Corrections:

1. You may have relaxed your arms. *Keep your arms tight next time!*

2. You may have looked back with your head first, causing the arms to create an angle between your arms and torso. *Keep your arms in stretch position and your head firmly between your arms.*

3. You may have bent your knees just before your hands contacted the mat. *The obvious solution: keep your legs straight until your hands contact the mat. The not so obvious solution: your quadriceps muscles may be too tight. This lack of flexibility forces the knees to bend to allow you the ability to get your hands down. Work on better quadriceps flexibility!*

Lack of shoulder and/or upper back flexibility. *Practice more shoulder flexibility drills!* Consult your coach for specific stretching exercises appropriate to your needs.

6 – Bridge: Wall Drills
(Secret 11)

The best way to set up these drills (in the gym) is to take an 8" landing cushion, which is usually 5-feet wide and 8-feet long and flip it up against the wall (5' high side). Make sure it safely and securely positioned.

- ### Drill: Walking down (and up) the wall.

Purpose: Now you begin the active process of reaching backwards for the floor, so you can feel the body positions you transition through to get to a bridge position.

Directions: Stand a distance away from the landing cushion that is roughly equal to the length of your legs from your heels to your hips.

From a stretch position, you reach backward, keeping your head in neutral position until your hands contact the mat. Once your hands are in contact with the mat you carefully walk down the wall to a bridge position.

From the bridge position, you can reverse directions and walk back up the wall and pull through your stomach to finish back in a standing stretch position.

Now, that you have an idea what it feels like to walk down the wall, you are now going to have the chance to work on reaching into a bridge position from a stand.

- **Drill: Reach down the wall with both hands** (with a spot).

Purpose: To learn how to reach backwards into a bridge position.

Directions: (Use an 8" landing cushion against the wall.) Stand a distance equal to the length of your legs away from the landing cushion, with your back to the cushion. Your spotter (someone of at least equal weight, height, and enough strength to control your body, preferably your coach) can stand at your side with one arm across your hips to help control your body as you reach backwards.

The focus on this drill is to keep your head in between your arms[23]. Do not look back with your head first or you will create an angle between your arms and your upper

---

[23] A back handspring, even a back walkover is really a blind element – meaning you don't see the floor before your hands make contact.

body, which is a weak position to be in when doing a back handspring.

Carefully reach back with both hands at the same time toward the landing cushion. The idea is to reach as far down the mat as you can in successive steps or attempts until you can effectively reach all the way to the floor on your own (see illustrations pp. 51 & 53).

Note: The spotter should support your hips until you are in a secure position on the mat or down on the floor.

- ### Drill: Bridge kick to handstand.

Purpose: To learn how to kick the legs one at a time up and into a handstand position with help from the abdominals, hip flexors, and shoulder muscles.

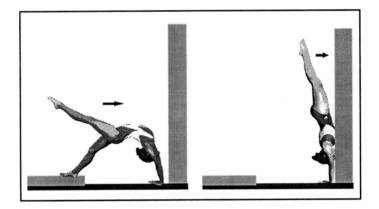

Directions: You push up into a bridge position with your hands right next to the 8" mat. Once in the bridge you must push back out of your legs until your shoulders are directly over your hands. Maintaining this position, you will now kick one leg up at a time, also pulling through abdominals and hip flexor muscles until you can finish in a handstand position with the front of your body flat up against the mat.

Note: You may find that a lack of strength, shoulder flexibility, experience, or any combination of these factors prevents you from doing this drill (see "Bridge kick over from panel mat" for help with this problem).

- **Drill: Bridge on wedge to kick over**

Purpose: To learn how to pull the lower body up and into a handstand position by using the abdominals, hip flexors, and shoulder muscles with a little help from the legs kicking up and over to a stand one at a time.

Directions: Place a wedge mat with the high end firmly against the wall. Push up into a bridge position so your feet are positioned halfway up the wedge, then shift your weight toward your shoulders and arms while pushing off slightly with one leg and lifting the other leg up and over through a split position. Step out through an arabesque.

- ## Drill: Bridge pull to handstand.

Purpose: To learn how to pull the lower body up and into a handstand position by using the abdominals, hip flexors, and shoulder muscles.

Directions: You push up into a bridge position with your hands right next to the 8" mat. Once in the bridge you must push back out of your legs until your shoulders are directly over your hands. Maintaining this position, you will now pull through abdominals and hip flexor muscles until you can finish in a handstand position with the front of your body flat up against the mat.

- ### Drill: Limber pull to handstand

(see "Drill: Reach Back to Bridge on Wedge Mat" on page 51 as a lead up to this drill.)

Purpose: To learn how to reach back into a limber safely from a standing stretch position and learn how to pull the lower body up and into a handstand position by using the abdominals, hip flexors, and shoulder muscles

Directions: Standing on an 8" landing cushion, with spotters ready to support you, if necessary, stretch through your fingertips, keeping your head in neutral position, and reach back and downward until your hands contact the landing cushion and you are in a controlled bridge position. Transfer your weight from your hips and your feet to your shoulders and your hands. Next, pull through your abdominal and hip flexor muscles, simultaneously pushing back and out of your shoulders until you have pulled your legs up to a handstand position.

- ## **Drill: Limber pull to handstand, snap down to push up position**

Purpose: This drill is almost like a slow motion back handspring. I say almost because a limber is a flexibility move that is done more or less in place, whereas a back handspring is meant to travel across the mat to pick up speed and power.

Directions: Standing on an 8" landing cushion, with spotters ready to support you, if necessary, stretch through your fingertips, keeping your head in neutral position, and reach back and downward until your hands contact the landing cushion and you are in a controlled bridge position.

Transfer your weight from your hips and your feet to your shoulders and your hands. Next, pull through your abdominal and hip flexor muscles, simultaneously pushing back and out of your shoulders until you have pulled your legs up to and through a handstand position from which you snap down to finish in a push up position on the mat.

"Coach Rik, why would you teach us something that could cause bad habits?"

That is a very good question and the answer is important to understand.

The Progression of Technique

In gymnastics, acrobatics, and tumbling, most skills are variations of **the core or foundation skills: forward roll, backward roll, handstand, and cartwheel.**

In gymnastics, the Balance Beam event is simply the perfection of floor skills performed four feet up in the air on a surface that is four-inches wide. A run punch to flyspring on the floor is similar to vault except in each stage of vault you transition to higher surfaces. Vault is simply tumbling up hill. A round off entry vault (Yurchenko) is a perfect demonstration of uphill tumbling.

While every event has elements of swing, an arm circling about the body, or legs circling on the floor (Thomas Flairs) the Uneven Bars for women is the only event that primarily focuses on swing. The gymnast's whole body swings through arcs of a circle (glide kips) or complete circles (giants).

Your coach must take the four basic tumbling skills and adapt them to a particular skill by changing:

- your angle of takeoff;
- your speed of motion;
- the swing of an arm or leg;
- your body size or shape (tuck, pike, straddle);
- and, the number of lines created by your body to make the technique successful for just you.

Your coach may have to alter that technique for other athletes based on their capabilities, which, other than physical characteristics many times is centered on physical conditioning.

Isn't it funny how everything keeps coming back to physical conditioning as a main component for success?

What is important for you to know is that while **bridges, back bends, and back walkovers are great drills for teaching awareness** and making you comfortable; each of these skills trains you to focus on flexibility rather than power. On a back walkover you reach back slowly, using the flexibility in your back and shoulders and barely travel any distance down the mat.

When you do a back handspring correctly, you will cover distance with speed and power. In fact, as you learn to do one, then two, then three back handsprings in a row; each handspring should get progressively faster and more powerful setting you up for somersaulting and other advanced tumbling skills.

So, in the beginning, a back walkover is good. Once you have overcome your fear of going backwards, you should set the back walkovers and bridges aside for a while (except as a warm up skill) and focus on the back handspring techniques. Consult with your coach to make sure you are prepared to move to the next level.

Always Focus on Safety!

7 - Fall Back Drills
(Secret 12)

Practice the following drills with a qualified gymnastics instructor first before practicing them on your own.

- ### Drill: Straight body fall back onto Port-a-pit
  (or stack of landing cushions)

  Purpose: To allow you to get used to falling backwards without fear of injury and to train you to keep your body aligned properly (I.E. stop looking over your shoulder, or turning your body in the beginning phase of a back handspring).

  Directions: Stand, just in front of a twenty-four inch (or higher) port-a-pit, in stretch position with your head in neutral and your fingers curled slightly forward. The idea is for you to fall backwards without bending hips, knees, or elbows and land flat on your back on the mat. If your body is tight, you may bounce a little but it shouldn't hurt at all. **Keep your lower back rounded throughout the fall.**

Important Safety Warning: It is extremely important that you keep your head in neutral position! If you look back for the mat or your head is sticking out when you land, you may cause serious injury to your neck or spine.

In addition, if you land with your fingers reaching backwards you can also cause a serious strain or possibly some broken finger bones. Follow these directions carefully.

- **Alternate Drill 1: Straight body fall back onto landing cushion with wedge underneath.**

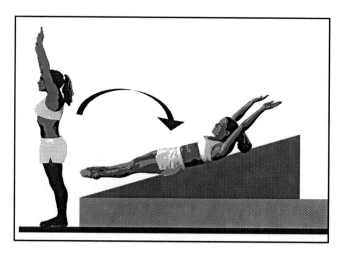

Perform this drill the same as the previous drill except the landing area is composed of a wedge mat with an 8" landing cushion underneath or you can put the landing cushion on top of the wedge – whichever is most comfortable. You will start the drill from the low end of the inclined matting and fall backward toward the raised end of the mat / wedge combination.

- ## **Alternate Drill 2: Straight body fall back into loose foam pit with 8" landing cushion on top of foam.**

Before beginning this drill, make sure the foam in the pit is sufficiently fluffed so it comes to floor level. If the foam is too low in the pit your body will continue to rotate as you fall causing you to land with most of the weight/force of the fall on your head and neck which could lead to serious injury.

"Coach Rik? Why are you always talking about the possibility of injury? Sometimes you make it sound scary."

I wish there was another way, but safety is just too important to leave to chance. If I can identify any way you might get hurt, it is my job to warn you.

I want you and every reader of this book to learn how to do a back handspring safely and successfully.

I don't want to scare anybody, but I do want to warn them of possible dangers.

Safety is no accident.

- ## **Alternate Drill 3: Fall back into spotters arms.**

Directions: The same as above except this time you will be landing in the arms of your spotter(s).

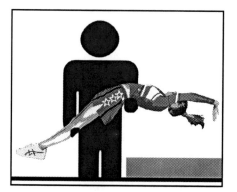

REALLY IMPORTANT POINT!

Your spotter must be strong enough to catch you safely when you fall backwards. Asking your Smurf-like cousin Myrtle to spot you will end up with a squished Myrtle and an injured you. My preference is that you ask a qualified gymnastics or cheer coach to spot you. Even then, make sure the person you pick is in good shape and plenty strong to catch you.

- **Drill: Fall back over foam barrel to handstand, snap down to push up position.**

The most important thing you need to do on this drill is make sure the barrel height is set appropriate for your body type. Some athletes have long legs, some have short legs and longer torso's. When performing this fall back drill over a foam barrel, you want your rear end to land on the barrel just before or right at the peak of the barrel. Two athletes of the same height but different physical builds may set this drill different from each other.

If the barrel is not set properly, it may give you little or no support, which doesn't make for a pleasant landing. **Consult with your gymnastics, cheer, or tumbling coach for the proper set up.**

Purpose: With back bends, bridges, and limbers you learned where you were upside-down. The initial fall back drills helped you overcome your innate fear of falling backwards and getting hurt. Now, you are going to add the awareness of reaching and falling backwards with controlled speed of motion.

Directions: Start in a standing stretch position and reach back slightly with your upper body allowing yourself to fall backwards over the barrel. As soon as your hands contact the 8" landing cushion begin pushing out of your shoulders and pulling with your abdominal and hip flexor muscles to move past the handstand position and snap down into a push up position.

Always Focus on Safety!

8 - Jump Back Drills
(Secret 13)

Now that you have had the chance to practice the Awareness Drills (I.E. bridge drills on the floor & wall, and the fall back drills) it is time to add power to your drills. As you may recall in the section titled *"The Progression of Technique"* (page 60), I told you that I may start you with a particular technique or drill that helps to emphasize one aspect of your future goal; the back handspring. When that technique has outlived its usefulness, which means you are progressing nicely, then it is time to move on to a more advanced drill or technique.

So, if both you and your coach feel you are ready, let's move on to the next drill.

- **Drill: Jump back to flat back landing on port-a-pit.[24]**

Purpose: A back handspring is a power move, not a flexibility move like a back walkover. You are now going to learn how to go backwards with explosive power out of your legs.

---

[24] Rather than continually repeating that you can substitute a port-a-pit with three or four stacked 8" landing mats, I will ask you to make the assumption, unless otherwise stated, that for training purposes a port-a-pit equals three to four-8" landing mats (secured and stabilized) depending on size, strength, & ability of the athlete.

Warning!
Land with a rounded lower back. This athlete shows too much arch.

Directions: Set up a stack of 8-inch landing cushions –at least three high- and make sure to fasten them together in some fashion so the mats do not slide, or use a thirty-six inch high (or higher) port-a-pit.

You will stand in a stretch position about two feet away from the mat (the mat is behind you!). Keep your arms straight and next to your ears; your upper body in line with your arms; allow your body to start falling backwards while bending your knees, and then explode out of your legs and jump back backwards to land in a stretched body position on the mats (port-a-pit) on your back.

IMPORTANT: Every time you practice this drill, remember to keep your head between your arms and your fingers curled slightly forward. Just like in the "fall back drill" you could seriously injure your head, neck, or fingers if you throw them backwards during this drill.

Note to Spotter: Keep a hand on the gymnast's head and neck on her first few attempts to make sure she keeps her head in neutral position during the drill.

- ## Drill: Jump back from panel mat to land on wedge

Purpose: To test leg power on each jump and to establish a *"no landing zone"* between the panel mat and the port-a-pit.

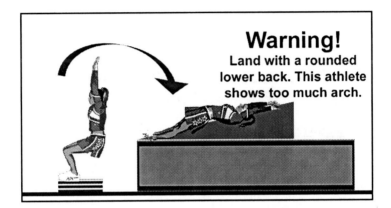

Warning!
Land with a rounded lower back. This athlete shows too much arch.

Directions: Place a panel mat one to two feet away from the port-a-pit and practice the jump back drill as described above. After each turn, move the panel mat three inches farther away from the port-a-pit/wedge. The goal is to see how far away from the port-a-pit/wedge you can jump from and still land safely with at least three-quarters of your body on the port-a-pit/wedge in a nice hollow body position.

I will often list a port-a-pit as the desired landing mat, because it is usually about 36-inches tall, and 8'X12' in width and length; a safe and practical mat for use in these drills. Not all gyms will have this equipment, however, many gyms do have several 8" landing mats which can be stacked one on top of the other and are adequate for these drills. Secure and stabilize these mats so they do not shift or move during the attempt at the skill. As with any piece of equipment, check that it is properly set before each attempt at the skill or drill. Consult with your gymnastics / cheer coach for specifics.

Remember: No arm swings, no bending forward, no squirming like a worm on landing to get more distance!

Review: Fall back over barrel to handstand.

Before attempting the jump back over the barrel, it is always a good idea to practice the fall back drill over the barrel again as a way of reacquainting you with what it feels like to go over the barrel with the feeling of partial support.

- ### Drill: Jump back over barrel to handstand; snap-down to push up position.

Purpose: To help you overcome the fear of jumping backwards to a handstand position, and then learning how to punch out of your shoulders and chest to snap down to a push up position.

Directions: Place an 8" landing cushion on the floor exercise mat with a large foam barrel on top of it at one end. Stand about one-foot away from the barrel in stretch position, and then bend your knees and explosively jump out of your legs while reaching back with your upper body over the barrel to land in a handstand position on the 8" landing cushion. Upon contact with the landing cushion, snap down into a push up position by blocking out of your shoulders and continuing to pull the lower body over using hip flexors and abdominal muscles.

Safety Note: Leave enough room (properly matted) behind the landing cushion in case your landing from the snap down takes you past the end of the first cushion.

Barrel Height

Special Note: For safety and proper training, the barrel should be of a height so the top of the barrel is in line with your lower back, right about where your tailbone is located, at the peak of your jump back.[25] The reason for this is what I call the Goldilocks Theory:

- If the barrel is too small, you may miss it entirely and land in a nose pose on the other side, or you will jump up and then fall straight down onto the barrel making a jerky motion rather than a graceful arc back to a handstand position.

- If the barrel is too big, every time you jump backward you do not make it up and over so the barrel stops rolling with you on top or it rolls back the way you came and you end up on the panel mat again.

- When the barrel is just the right size, you will jump backward in a graceful arc and the barrel will temporarily support your weight as you roll to the handstand position.

---

[25] This may be a different height setting from the fall back over the barrel drill since now you are adding the power of the jump.

You can adjust your height relative to the barrel by:

- adding to your height with the use of a panel mat;

- Unfolding a panel mat halfway and putting it under the barrel on top of the landing cushion;

- Double the height of the landing cushion;

- Use a smaller / bigger barrel;

Barrel Distance
(determined by individual athlete's needs)

If you are barely making it over the barrel, it may be too far away; if you are almost missing the barrel you may need to move it farther away.

The idea is to have the barrel support you just enough to help you make it safely. If all your weight is on the barrel, then you are not working hard enough. If you are barely touching the barrel and making it over successfully, it may be time for you to move on to higher level techniques!

Consult with your coach to determine the proper set up of matting to do this drill correctly.

* * *

Barrel Spotting:

Several of the drills in this book make use of the barrel as a teaching / spotting device for learning back handsprings. While you are practicing your back handsprings over the barrel, it is a good idea to have a spotter controlling the barrel.

Each attempt at a back handspring may have variations Having a qualified spotter who can roll the barrel closer or farther away as needed will help speed the learning process. Every athlete learning to do a back handspring should take turns learning to use the barrel, always under the supervision of a qualified gymnastics or cheer coach, to help fellow athletes learn a back handspring safely.

Review: Fall back drill with spotter.

- ### Drill: Jump back drill with spotter

Purpose: To develop your confidence in working with a spotter on this skill.

Directions: (with a spotter standing or kneeling at your side) Start in stretch position, and then as you begin to lean backwards, bend your knees almost 90° and then explode out of your legs backward and drive your upper body back and into a handstand allowing your spotter to guide and support you as necessary.

I think responsible and safety-focused athletes in their teens can learn how to spot a back handspring. The more you spot, the more you will understand the mechanics of the skill (i.e. how things work). Begin the process of learning to spot with a mentor, preferably a qualified gymnastics or cheer coach. Only spot gymnasts similar in size to yourself or smaller.

You must be 100% confident you have the strength and ability to control the athlete you are spotting. Their lives are literally in your hands! Double spot with your coach until he / she says you may spot another athlete by yourself.

- **Drill: Back handspring in a Spotting Belt**
  (on a trampoline or the floor)

Many gyms have a device called an "overhead spotting rig" which is usually set up over a large trampoline. The device consists of a belt, which is tightly fastened around your waist that has metal rings on either side of it. Ropes are attached to the rings and routed through pulleys mounted to ceiling brackets. The ends of both ropes eventually come together in your coach's hands so he can spot you while standing beside the tramp.

Your coach can keep you suspended in the air by pulling down on the ropes to keep your from landing on your head. Experienced coaches will use minimal support to allow you to accomplish as much of the skill as you can by yourself.

Using an overhead spotting rig is an art in itself and should only be used by qualified gymnastics, cheer, or tumbling coaches.

- **Drill: Back Handspring down the Wedge** (with spot)

    <u>Purpose:</u> Not only is the wedge a safe mat to practice on but it adds the helping hand of gravity to the effort since you are practicing the skill in a downhill direction.

Directions: (with a coach spotting at your side) Start in stretch position, and then as you begin to lean backwards, bend your knees almost 90° and then explode out of your legs backward while driving your upper body back and into a handstand, allowing your spotter to guide and support you as necessary, and then snap down to a stand. As you progress in confidence and competence, your coach can stand by for a safety spot, and when you are finally ready, your coach will step aside and let you do the back handspring on your own down the incline mat – and when that happens...

Congratulations!
Pat yourself on the back for a job well done.

Always Focus on Safety!

9 - Punch and Hollow Body Drills
(Secret 14)

So far, I have been letting you practice back handsprings from a bent knee jump and that is really a bad habit – if your goal is more advanced tumbling.

Jumping versus Punching

You began your journey of movement skills in life first by rocking from side to side, or back and forth, pretty soon you started to crawl, eventually walk, then run, and a special few of you have added other extraordinary abilities like tumbling, dancing, cheerleading, ice skating and several other artistic expressions using the human body.

The metaphor holds for training in gymnastics, tumbling, and acrobatics; you started with rolls, then handstands, then cartwheels until now you are working on what is practically the core skill for all advanced tumbling – the back handspring.

In a similar way, I presented you with the techniques of a back handspring by starting from the simpler movements and then made them progressively more difficult as you increased in competence and confidence.

You started off with back bends and bridges, then fall back drills, followed by jump back drills, **until now** when your focus on snap-down drills requires you to keep your legs straight during the performance of the skill; bent legs will ruin the drill completely.

Force, in this case, the power of your body in motion, travels in a straight line, or in the case of a back handspring, a slightly arched line.

Have you ever bounced on a trampoline? What happens when you bend your legs when landing from a bounce on the trampoline? That's right; it kills your bounce – literally stops your bounce as soon as you land on the tramp. The same thing happens when you bend your knees on a vault springboard; it kills your punch (bounce / rebound) off the board.

What is a spring floor? Basically, it's a modified version of a trampoline or springboard. Under the carpet, foam, and boards are hundreds of springs or specialized foam blocks[26] designed to spring you back into the air in equal proportion to the power of your punch on takeoff.

Bending your knees on takeoff redirects the force of your punch in directions that are of no help in completing a successful back handspring.

Think about it. If you were standing straight up and down on the trampoline and started to bounce, what would happen?

"You would go straight up in your bounce."

Correct. Now, what would happen if you bent your legs the next time you landed on the trampoline?

---

[26] Advanced acrobats use a "ski floor."

"It would immediately stop my bounce."

Again, you are correct. To summarize, punching is when you take off from the floor with straight, tight legs allowing the floor to rebound or bounce you back into the air like a tramp bed or a spring board. Jumping off the floor is when you bend your knees and only use the internal power of your muscles – not as efficient as punching.

As you move into the snap down drills, it is important that you focus on punching out of both your arms and legs to complete the techniques correctly.

Punch Drills (shoulders & chest and legs)

This is the first time you will add power to any of the drills. The most important thing to understand is the difference between a snap down and a pike down.

In some of the fall-back drills over the barrel, your instruction was to land with your body in a push up position. This was to keep you from developing the bad habit of piking down to a stand versus snapping down to a stand through your chest and shoulders.

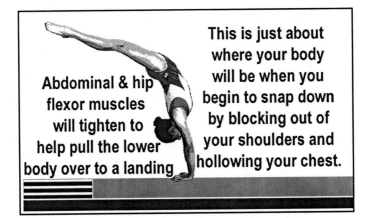

Abdominal & hip flexor muscles will tighten to help pull the lower body over to a landing

This is just about where your body will be when you begin to snap down by blocking out of your shoulders and hollowing your chest.

In a later drill when you actually jump backwards and land in a handstand position, your shoulders and chest will be put into a stretched and slightly arched position. It is at this point where the snap through; the sudden punching out of the shoulders and hollowing of the chest occurs (see the illustration at the top of the next page).

Legs

- ### Drill: Multiple rebound drill on a spring board.

Purpose: To help you understand the difference between punching and jumping.

Directions: Stand on a springboard with both hands placed on the Vault Table or a wall in front of you or a spotter may hold your hands. Bend your knees and take one jump up, and then punch off the board ten times in a row bouncing as high as you can while still maintaining control of the bounce.

If you keep your legs straight you will continuously rebound; if you bend them once, you will immediately stop bouncing – in other words kill the power of the skill, just like you do when you bend your knees tumbling on the floor.

Shoulders and Chest Drill

- ### Underarm reach to handstand with a shoulder block off the floor.

Purpose: To develop shoulder block. This drill is borrowed from vaulting where block through the shoulders is essential for developing a powerful vault.

Directions: Standing in stretch position, with your arms next to your ears, step forward while at the same time driving your upper body forward / downward to reach forcefully into a stretched handstand position on the floor. Upon contact with the floor, immediately punch out your shoulders and hollow your chest so your body briefly rises into the air and then you land back in the handstand position.

The blocking action off the floor is similar to doing a shoulder shrugging motion with both arms above your head.

- **Drill: Punch through chest with springboard**

Purpose: To learn how to punch through the chest forcefully to help with the blocking action of the upper body during a back handspring.

Warning! Locked elbows could lead to injury.

Directions: Lean a vault spring board up against a wall (where it will do no damage!) You will place your hands, shoulder-width apart, on the springboard so a ninety-degree angle forms between your arms and body. Your lower back should remain rounded with the hips tucked under and the stomach sucked in tight.

Your arms must stay straight throughout this drill, however, it is important that you keep your hands turned in slightly in case you need to bend your elbows to stop the drill. **Note:** Adjust the number of springs in the board to the athlete's ability.

The only movement will be the chest relaxing forward, and then quickly hollowing so the shoulders are rounded which will cause the upper body to come off the board.

Your spotter will stand directly behind you and push you back (carefully!) toward the springboard. Keeping your arms straight and tight, you will once again quickly punch through the chest and block off the board. The goal is to do this drill 5 to 10 times in a row in rapid succession.

> **IMPORTANT:** The spotter must be of a size and physical condition that he/she can easily spot / catch you as you rapidly rebound off the board.

The combination of the shoulder block and punching through the chest is how the accomplished tumbler blocks off the floor to single or multiple back handsprings.

Hollow Body Drills

- **Drill: Log roll between mats.**

Purpose: To develop your ability to keep the shoulders, hips, and torso tight during the performance of a skill or drill. If your arms are tight and your legs are tight but you are loose in the stomach or lower back, the power of your punch will still be absorbed.

Directions: You will need four folded panel mats for this drill. Place two panel mats end to end on the floor, and then place the other two panel mats end to end on the floor parallel to the first set of mats. The two lines of panel mats should be two to three feet apart.

To begin this drill you will lie down with your feet on one set of mats and your arms and shoulders on the other set of mats.

The idea is to lift your hips up off the floor and roll the length of the mats without relaxing or allowing any part of your body to touch the floor between the mats.

When you can successfully roll down the mats in one direction begin rolling back up the mats in the opposite direction.

This is an excellent drill for teaching hollow-body tightness.

- ## Drill: Reach back from knees, pull through to kneeling stretch position.

Purpose: Most of the drills to this point for the torso have focused on the hip flexors and lower to mid-abdominal muscles. This drill focuses more on the upper range of the abdominal muscles, which makes it a really good drill for front handsprings and front somersaults, but it is still peripherally helpful for follow through in the full range of motion for the snap-down action of your upper body in tandem with the blocking action out of the chest and shoulders.

Note: The gymnast pictured in the illustration should have her head between her arms.

Directions: Start in a kneeling "stretch position" with your knees approximately shoulder-width apart for stability. You can start this drill in front of an 8" landing mat placed against the wall, so your toes are just touching the mat and your body is the distance of your lower leg away from the mat/wall. Stretch up and out of your shoulders while reaching back with your whole upper torso to lightly touch your fingers to the mat against the wall, and then, pull through your upper-abdominal muscles, to return to a kneeling stretch position.

Next, place a folded panel mat directly in back of your toes and reach back to lightly touch the mat and then pull through to the start position again.

If you have really good flexibility and exceptional upper-abdominal strength, you may be able to do this drill on the floor exercise carpet with no additional matting, however, it would be prudent to have a spotter nearby to help – just in case.

Combining Punch & Pull Through Abdominals

- **Drill: Reach back, punch & pull through to standing stretch position on incline mat.**

Purpose: Again, this drill will work the upper region of your abdominal muscles, but you are also going to add a light punch/block out of your shoulders to get your first taste of falling (controlled) backward and anticipating the landing on the wall so you can immediately block out of your chest and shoulders. Use a spotter on this drill until you have developed a high degree of confidence and competence..

Directions: *(Use a spotter with this skill.)* Place an incline mat up against a padded / matted wall. Start a distance away from the wall that is roughly twice the distance of your lower leg – adjust as necessary.

Stretch up and out of your shoulders while reaching back with your whole upper torso and allow yourself to fall the short distance to the wall. Upon contact, immediately block out of your chest and shoulders while pulling through your upper abdominal muscles to return to a standing position. Maintain an open shoulder angle throughout the drill.

- ### Drill: Pac man punch off wall.

Purpose: To create a closer simulation of the back handspring motion to teach you how to block out of your shoulders for the snap-down portion of the skill.

Directions: Place an 8" landing mat up against the wall with a spotting block, trapezoid segment, or panel mat adjusted in height and width to the needs of the athlete. This block is a necessary component of the set up that keeps the Pac man-shaped barrel from rolling all the way into the wall, which could smoosh you between mat and barrel. Adjust this set up based on your height and arm length so your hands contact the mat / padded wall just before the foam barrel would contact the 24-inch high block.

Start by sitting on the Pac man barrel (with your feet on a folded up panel mat if necessary) so from the bottom of your seat to your fingertips, your upper body is one stretched line. Push out of your legs while immediately extending your body and holding a tight, slightly stretched body line. When your hands contact the mat / padded wall, immediately block out of your shoulders and roll forward. When your feet contact the folded panel mat, you may return to a seated position on the Pac man barrel. Repeat this drill several times in a row. Have a qualified spotter nearby to help guide you and the barrel as necessary.

- ## Drill: The Sisyphus Drill[27]

Purpose: Similar to the "Pac man punch off wall" drill, this is a variation that makes you work a bit harder and rotates your body to a near handstand position that is quite similar to the feel of doing a back handspring.

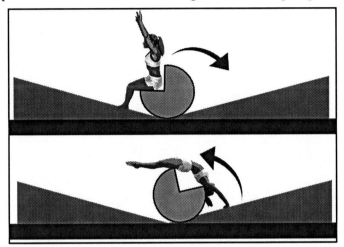

Sit on the Pac man barrel so from hips to fingertips your upper body is one stretched line. Push out of your legs while immediately extending your body and holding a tight, slightly stretched body line. When your hands contact the incline mat, immediately block out of your shoulders and roll forward. When your feet contact the opposite incline mat, you may return to a seated position on the Pac man barrel. Repeat this drill several times in a row. Have a qualified spotter nearby to help guide you and the barrel as necessary.

---

[27]Sisyphus, in Greek mythology, king of Corinth, the son of Aeolus, king of Thessaly. Sisyphus saw the god Zeus carry off the beautiful maiden Aegina and told her father what he had witnessed. Enraged with Sisyphus, Zeus condemned him to Tartarus, where he was compelled for eternity to roll to the top of a steep hill a stone that always rolled down again. Microsoft ® Encarta ® Encyclopedia 2005. © 1993-2004 Microsoft Corporation. All rights reserved.

Always Focus on Safety!

10 - Snap Down Drills
(Secret 15)

The last chapter focused on tight body at the handstand / snap-down position. You will quickly find that any looseness in your body will significantly rob you of the power necessary to make a back handspring not only easier to do but a lot more fun than landing in a nose pose on the floor! The focus of this section is on snap-down drills from the handstand position to immediate rebound into a...

- **Drill: Snap down to flat back on Port-a-Pit (or stack of 8" mats).**

Purpose: To connect the snap down and rebound to flat back in one motion.

Directions: Stack two to four panel mats on the floor at one end of the tumble tramp, and stack four 8" landing mats or one Port-a-pit approximately ¾ of the length of your body away from the stacked panel mats on top of the Tumble Tramp (see illustration).

IMPORTANT: Place a landing mat on the floor in back and to the sides of the stacked panel mats in case you kick up too high and fall over or to the side. Other gymnasts waiting their turn should be standing off to the side of the tumble tramp.

Directions: Standing with your back to the port-a-pit, take one or two bounces to get up to a ¾ handstand on the stacked mats, and then, snap down through the chest and shoulders so your feet land just in front of your body. Keep your legs tight so the tramp will immediately rebound or bounce you at an angle up and backwards so you land on your back (slightly rounded) on the port-a-pit keeping your head in neutral position and your arms next to your ears (fingers curled slightly forward).

The sensation of snapping down to the tumble tramp may feel uncomfortable the first few times, causing you to bend your knees, which will immediately kill your bounce. If this is the case, practice taking one or two small bounces from a standing position, then on the third bounce lean back slightly so the tramp propels your body backward causing you to land on your back on the port-a-pit as described above.

VERY IMPORTANT: Always keep your head in a neutral position when rebounding backwards to prevent severe injury to your head or neck on landing! In addition, keep your fingers rounded slightly forward so they don't get bent backwards causing potential discomfort or injury.

- **<u>Drill: Snap down from ¾ handstand to BHS over barrel to stand 8" landing cushion.</u>** (on Tumble Tramp with a spotter)

<u>Purpose:</u> To help you develop the feeling for connecting the motions of the snap-down directly to the punch and subsequent handstand position with no delays or false starts.

<u>Set up:</u> Two to four panel mats stacked or a spotting block on the end of the tumble tramp on the floor. A foam barrel on top of an 8" landing mat three to four feet away from the stack of mats (adjust distance according to your height and power).

<u>Spotting Note:</u> A spotter should control the barrel. If you land short, the spotter can roll the barrel forward underneath you. If you jump too far, the spotter can roll the barrel out until it is under your hips. If your power fizzles on top and you get stuck like a broken down Ferris wheel, your spotter can help roll you over to a finish position.

For the first few attempts, start from a stand, take one bounce, and then do the back handspring over the barrel landing in a push up position on the mat. Once you are comfortable, continue with the following directions.

Directions: Just like the snap down to a flat back on the port-a-pit you will take one or two bounces to a ¾ handstand and then snap down with tight legs onto the tramp bed; landing with both feet well in front of your body. Your body position on landing should be rounded hollow position with tight muscles. The tramp bed will first absorb the power of the snap down, and then it will spring back with equal power launching your body up and backwards.

Your goal is to drive your upper torso, not your head and arms, but your whole upper torso with your arms extended and next to your ears, up and backward over the barrel. When your hands contact the 8" landing mat you will snap down to a stand.

Repeat this process one million times or until you can make it to the handstand snap down on the landing mat without the use of the barrel.

- ### Drill: [floor] Snap down to BHS over Barrel.

Purpose: to help you get a feel for the timing and body tension needed to do a snap down BHS on a spring floor.

Set up: Two or three panel mats stacked (depending on your height and strength); an 8" landing mat with a foam barrel placed at the end nearest the stacked panel mats; and, a qualified spotter.

Directions: Kick up one leg at a time to a ½ or ¾ handstand, and then snap down and land with both feet well in front of your body. Your body position on landing should be a rounded hollow position with tight muscles.

Like the tramp bed, but not as spongy, the spring floor will absorb the power of the snap down, and then it will spring back with equal power launching your body up and backwards. **Note:** The spring floor is not forgiving of bent legs so stay very tight.

Drive your upper torso with your arms extended and next to your ears, up and backward over the barrel. When your hands contact the 8" landing mat you will snap down to either a push up position or a stand on the mat depending on your ability to block out of your chest and shoulders.

- **Drill: [floor] Snap down to BHS onto 8" landing cushion.**

Purpose: To get the feel of transitioning from the snap-down immediately to a back handspring without the support of a foam barrel.

Set up: Two or three panel mats stacked (depending on your height and strength); an 8" landing mat and a qualified spotter.

Directions: Kick up one leg at a time to a ½ or ¾ handstand, and then snap down and land with both feet well in front of your body. Your body position on landing should be a rounded hollow position with tight muscles. On rebounding from the floor, drive your upper body predominantly backward to land in a handstand position on the 8" landing cushion and follow through to a snap-down to a stand. Ask a qualified gymnastics or cheer coach to spot your initial attempts. When the coach says you are ready, you can do it on your own.

Note: This drill is also easily performed on the tumble tramp (with a spotter!) – the key word being "easily." Once you are capable of doing the back handspring on the floor competently and with bucket loads of confidence, it may be a good idea to continue practicing the back handspring in the workout gear that most closely matches what you will typically wear while performing the skill (I.E. cheer outfit with sneakers, martial arts uniform, dance outfit, or leotard).

Once you are comfortable performing the skill in your normal performance wear, you can begin practicing the skill in the environment where you will most often perform it. Always start with matting and progress toward the "performance environment" under the supervision of a qualified gymnastics / cheer / tumbling coach.

Always Focus on Safety!

11 - Round Off: Key to Advanced Tumbling

(Secret 16)

> I have found for some athletes that it is quicker to teach the round off back handspring first. So after you have done the awareness, fall back, and jump back drills. With the guidance and qualified assessment of a gymnastics or cheer coach you may be able to bypass the standing back handspring and move right into the round off back handspring. Consult with your coach first!

Throwing yourself through the air on a wing and a prayer is the least effective method for doing a round off back handspring. Safety-wise, it is not an appropriate or helpful method of learning this skill.

Unfortunately, this method is all too common. Most often, what I see is a gymnast running down the mat, then setting up the skill with a high hurdle and turning her body in the air as if she is doing a ½ on twist to the vault table. This early turn of the upper body usually results in a tumbling pass that swerves off the diagonal tumbling pass on a crooked path.

I want you to promise to learn the round off correctly. Not only will it make the back handspring easier to do; it will make it more powerful, and it will become a great lead-up skill for adding back somersaults. Sure, some of your friends will be bragging about their (*seizure technique*) round off back handsprings, but in the long run, if you put in the effort now, you will be a significantly better tumbler than the other athletes who cut corners.

"Where did little cartwheels and round offs come from, Coach Rik?"

Popular gymnastics mythology would seem to indicate that cartwheels came from early acrobats imitating the motions of a wheel on a cart, which had two boards crossing each other around which a wheel was placed.

The first cartwheels were completely sideways. Later, the cartwheel became stylized somewhat in that the tumbler may start from a forward facing position, as though she was going to kick up to a handstand but at the last moment turned sideways to do a front to side cartwheel. Other times the tumbler started sideways but stepped down facing back the way she had come for a side to back cartwheel; still other tumblers combine all three positions and did front-side-back cartwheels. Eventually, and I am just guessing at this point, someone started a front side back cartwheel and accidentally finished with both feet together and the round off was born (*of course, I could be wrong*).

In any case, I am going to have you focus on learning a front-side-back cartwheel as the basis for a correct round off.

Front – Side – Back Cartwheels

- ## Drill: Kick to (front) Handstand to & from a T-position.

Purpose: To teach you that driving your upper body down into a round off is just like kicking into a handstand.

Directions: Starting in a stretch position on the floor, kick into a tight body handstand by moving through a T-position on the way up and as you step back down through an arabesque position to a stretch position.

- ## Drill: Side to side cartwheel [both sides]

Purpose: To develop control of the arms and legs while moving in a lateral or sideways movement pattern.

Set up: Place two or three 8" landing cushions up against the wall, securely fastened, so they don't fall down.

Directions: The objective is to do a cartwheel completely sideways – no turn out of the lead foot; keep your head in neutral (middle illustration incorrect); do not look in the direction of travel.

- **<u>Canyon drill:</u>** (fun drill)

With the 8" landing mats against the wall (as described above) create a canyon by sliding over a port-a-pit or stacks of panel mats that are higher than you waist. The idea is to do a completely sideways cartwheel in the canyon without touching the mats on either side. After each turn, you will move the mats a little closer together. You have mastered this skill when you can do a side to side cartwheel on the low beam. **<u>Note:</u>** Remember to work this and all cartwheel drills to both right and left sides.

It may be more difficult on your non-dominant side (uncomfortable side) but it will help with bilateral symmetry and possibly open additional bridges between the right and left hemispheres of your brain through the corpus callosum[28]. Don't worry about understanding this last paragraph; just pretend it's like vegetables, which are good for you. Eat your vegetables and do your cartwheels on both sides!

---

[28] The two cerebral hemispheres are partially separated from each other by a deep fold known as the longitudinal fissure. Communication between the two hemispheres is through several concentrated bundles of axons, called commissures, the largest of which is the corpus callosum. Microsoft ® Encarta ® Encyclopedia 2005 © 1993-2004 Microsoft Corporation. All rights reserved.

- ### Drill: Side to side cartwheel hold last leg at horizontal. [both sides]

Purpose: To teach you how to shift your weight from your upper body to your legs in a controlled manner.

Directions: The same as the side cartwheel except as the first foot steps down you will quickly lift the head and shoulders (staying sideways) until your weight is above your support leg and the opposite leg is held to the side in a horizontal position. It is important in this drill to keep the support leg straight and not allow the body to pivot. Practice this drill to both sides.

- ### Drill: Front to side cartwheel hold last leg up.

Purpose: To combine the "Front to Handstand," and "Side to Side," cartwheel drills.

Directions: The key to this drill is timing. You will kick up as though you are working on a handstand, however, when your fingertips are one inch from the floor you will quickly pivot your body sideways to finish as though you had done a side to side cartwheel [last leg held in horizontal position].

- **Drill: Front to side cartwheel; hold last leg in horizontal 1 second, and then pivot to backward finishing position pulling legs together and snapping chest upright.**

Purpose: To help you focus on the final pivot as this will become the snap down portion of the round off.

Directions: Do a front to side cartwheel as described above and hold the last leg at the horizontal position for one second, and then pivot your body by rotating on the ball of your support leg foot in the direction from which you have come while snapping the leg at horizontal down and together with your support leg.

- **Drill: Front-side-back cartwheel.**

Purpose: This drill is the culmination of the above drills. It is important that each phase of this drill is distinctly shown. Allowing the front side of this drill to blur into the side portion because you turn too early (more than one inch above the floor) will cause you to develop bad habits.

Directions: The same as the above drill except there will be no pause or hold of the leg; you will move through the skill showing each position but continue to move smoothly to the end, which is a stretch position.

Special Note: Before the second leg closes with the support leg, the head, chest, and arms should already be up in the stretch position. If you have done the skill correctly, you will find that finishing in this position correctly develops some power and may cause you to take a step or two backwards to control the kinetic energy from the momentum of the skill.

You may notice that I am not including the "run, hurdle, RO" as a drill because I want you to focus on technique and get away from the erroneous thinking that a fast run is necessary.

Importance of the Round Off

The round off is the transitional skill (transfers power from one element to another) from the run and hurdle to back handsprings, somersaults and several other skills. Yet, even with this all-important role the round off is easily one of the most neglected skills from a coaching standpoint.

The position of your body at the end of the snap down from the round off is crucial to the setup of the following skill. If you land with your feet in the "A" position, which is typical for many novice tumblers, you will most likely have little or no power for the next tumbling skill. If you are doing a back handspring from this position, you will most likely buckle your knees on takeoff or gain forward (cause your body to move forward rather than backward) which is not a good takeoff position for back handsprings or any other tumbling skill. The only way for you to get into a back handspring from the "A" position is to buckle (bend) your knees so you can get your center of gravity past the vertical position, which will allow you to travel backwards but will drastically reduce the power of the skill.

If you snap down with your feet closer to the "B" position, you will certainly transfer more power from the run and hurdle with nice tight legs and good stretch of the upper body, but you will tend to block upward with very little rotation of her body backward. *(At more advanced levels of tumbling, this position may be appropriate for setting somersaulting skills.)*

Moving into a back handspring from block angle "C" can still be a little scary. Although you may land straight up and down on the floor from the snap down of your round off, the horizontal force from takeoff or more forcefully from a hurdle and round off will cause your body to continue rotating backward – just a bit higher in the air than is normally recommended for a competent back handspring.

Block angle "D" would be the ideal takeoff position into the back handspring with straight, tight legs punching through the floor.[29]

The following drills emphasize the landing positions needed for training the rebound and for training the transition from round off to the back handspring.

- ### Drill: Round off rebound

Special Note: Once again, this is a skill that falls into the "good to demonstrate one aspect of a technique but not-so-good for the overall skill" category. The one aspect to get is a clean jump-hurdle to front-side-back style round off. (This is good training for a round off into a back tuck somersault.)

Purpose: To teach you that correct technique for a front-side-back round off may be initiated from a stand rather than from an out of control run across the floor.

---

29 "B" and to some degree "C" are standard takeoff positions for back somersaults. "C" is typical for novice gymnasts learning back tuck somersaults, although not necessarily ideal. "B" is a good position for setting layout somersaults when combined with a strong horizontal force from the run, hurdle, and round off or a takeoff from a similar position from a back handspring (see illustration page 106).

Directions: Jump from two feet to a hurdle and focus on entering this skill as though you are about to kick up to a handstand. When your hands are inches from the floor, pivot ¼ turn, and then pivot another ¼ turn at the handstand before squaring your hips to snap down, by blocking off the floor through your shoulders and chest to a hollow position.

In this instance, you do want to execute a controlled rebound that shows some amplitude, so snap down and land with your feet behind your body in position "B" *(see page 106).* The key is in lifting your head and chest quickly from the snap down so you are spotting something at eye level, which will help you to control your balance when landing from the rebound.

Note: This should be a rebound (punch off the floor) and not a bent knee jump into the rebound position.

Spotting/Safety Tip: The chance for over-rotation on the rebound is high for athletes new to this skill. Ask a qualified coach to spot you for possible over-rotation. Review safety landing drills, especially the backwards landing with "rock and roll" technique before practicing this skill on the floor exercise mat.

- **Drill: [From stretch position] One leg at horizontal; drive into F-S-B round off with rebound to stick position.**

Purpose: Similar to the last drill, but instead of a jump to a hurdle, you must now refine the technique even more to do it correctly. Running and jumping should not be a substitute for correct technique.

Directions: From a standing stretch position, you will lift one leg slightly above horizontal and then take a large step forward, driving the upper body down to the ground to initiate a front-side-back round off with a rebound to a stick landing position.

Note: Start this drill on a line on the floor to give yourself feedback about how straight you are tumbling. If you land off to one side or the other of the line, it is likely that you are turning too early in the front (or lead up to the handstand) portion of the round off. The lower you can drive your upper body in the handstand kick up portion of the drill, before pivoting your body sideways, the more square your body will be on the line at the finish of the skill. **Ask your coach to spot the rebound, if necessary.**

- **Drill: F-S-B-Round Off rebound to flat back landing on port-a-pit.**

Purpose: To learn the proper takeoff position and body tension to make the floor rebound your body during takeoff.

Set up: The same as the above drill except the port-a-pit is flat on the floor in front of one or two stacked panel mats (SPM's). **Use a spotter.**

Directions: Do a front side back round off over a stack of panel mats and snap down to the floor with your feet in front of your body. Open your body on the rebound from the floor to full extension so you can land flat on your back on top of the port-a-pit.

IMPORTANT: Upon landing on the port-a-pit, keep your head between your arms and your fingers slightly rounded otherwise, you could injure your neck or hurt your fingers.

- **Drill: Jump hurdle or 1 step F-S-B Round Off rebound to BHS on 8" landing cushion from panel mats [with a spot].**

Purpose: So you can learn how to combine the front-side-back round off with rebound into an immediate back handspring.

Set up: Two stacked panel mats with two 8" landing cushions placed end to end at the end of the panel mats.

Directions: From stacked panel mats do a front-side-back round off to immediate back handspring on an 8" landing cushion.

IMPORTANT: Have a qualified coach nearby to provide a safety spot.

- ### Drill: Snapdown 1, 2, or 3 back handsprings on tumble tramp

Practicing multiple back handsprings in a row on the tumble tramp (**with a spot, if necessary**) is also a good transition progression that allows you to feel the snap down motion straight into back handsprings.

- ### Drill: Snapdown 1, 2, or 3 back handsprings off springboard with spot

Once you have demonstrated appropriate skill and confidence performing multiple back handsprings on the tumble tramp, you can transition to the floor exercise mat and practice snapping down from the end of a springboard into 1, 2, or 3 back handsprings.

As in the transition from the round off to the back handspring, each snap down (from the springboard or preceding back handspring) that leads into another horizontally focused tumbling skill (across the floor) should finish with your feet landing in front of your body.

Spotting Tip: As the gymnast is snapping down from the springboard, place your hand on her lower back to provide support and, if need be, help guide her body backwards into the back handspring.

- ### Drill: Snapdown 1-2-3 back handsprings off panel mat on floor with spot

This drill is similar to the snap down drill from the springboard with the major exception that now you must really focus on a strong snap down through your chest and shoulders in order to land in a good take off position into the first back handspring. Poor positioning of the feet on the snap down to first back handspring virtually guarantees a tumbling pass with little or no power and minimal amplitude on the rebound.

Multi-Joint Patterning Exercise

Another great aspect to this drill is that it is a multi-joint patterning exercise. This skill requires every tumbler to use certain muscles (around specific joints) in a specific sequence and at an appropriate place and time to develop an effective tumbling pass.

By making this tumbling pass, in effect, an exercise you are training your muscles in a technique-specific pattern of movement. The number of tumbling passes you do is determined by your form and safety.

If your form breaks down, you will practice a bad habit, which will become more ingrained the more it is practiced incorrectly. Sloppy performance can also lead to accidents. Start slowly and build the number of passes you do each workout based on safety and quality of skill performance.

Skill: Round-Off Back Handspring

Purpose: This is the whole reason you bought this book. Your moment of glory is here! You made it!

Safety Note: Even after doing all these drills to get to this point, it is still a good idea to have a spotter the first time you do the whole combination.

<u>Directions:</u> From a jump hurdle, do a front-side-back round off landing with your feet in front of your body and immediately punch through the floor while driving your upper body backward / downward to momentarily pass through a handstand position from which you block through your shoulders and chest to snap-down and finish in a stretch position.

Congratulations! You may now officially jump for joy, hug your coach, show off for mom and dad, call Grandma with the good news, brag to your friends and try and explain this glorious feat to your dog (although he won't understand because he probably doesn't speak English).

You have now accomplished a skill sequence very few people in the world can brag about. To keep your timing and training up to date you must continue working out.

When you are ready to add to your collection of tumbling skills, visit **www.GymnasticsTrainingTips.com** for more information on advanced tumbling and techniques for other popular gymnastics skills. Besides, I would love to hear your success story!

Good luck and remember always focus on safety!

12 - The Back Handspring:
A Key to Success in Life?

Yes, a back handspring is a great metaphor and indicator for your continued success in life. Very few people who start to read a book actually follow through and finish the whole book[30] and the same may be true for those learning back handsprings or attempting any of several other goals they want to accomplish – very few follow through and finish.

That is why learning a back handspring is an excellent indicator of your future success in life. The best thing about learning a back handspring is that success only occurs because of the time and effort **you** put in to this goal.

In a world where many people expect to have, be, do, or achieve magnificent goals; they also expect the goals to be handed to them on a golden platter with virtually no effort on their part.

Other than your fairy godmother, who is probably a cast member from "Queer Eye for the Straight Guy," there is no coach, instructor, or parent who can wave a magic wand and give you a back handspring.

---

[30] Congratulations on making it this far.

YOU accomplished a back handspring by putting in continuous effort by:

- showing up for training day after day;

- improving your physical condition;

- learning new and different techniques from your mentors and coaches; and,

- frequent practice of these skills and drills.

All of which is a recipe for success that you can use in all areas of your life when modified to the goals you have chosen.

You have accomplished a skill beyond the powers of normal mortals. Go forth from this place and vow to use your powers for good, to achieve your goals, and to mentor others in the practical realities of personal success.

Always Focus on Safety!

<u>Appendix A: Basic Body Positions</u>

Tuck   Squat   Pike

Closed Pike   Straddle   Closed Straddle

Pike Stand   Forward Split   Bridge / Back Bend

Straddle Stand   Lunge   Stretch Position

Layout   Prone

Safety Responsibility

As I have stated, will state, and continuously harp on; Safety is no accident!

I seriously considered not writing this book until I realized that you make decisions daily which seriously affect your safety.

Simply crossing the road requires you to be aware of oncoming traffic and make the judgment of when it is safe to cross the road.

Recognizing "stranger danger" and even danger from people you know and getting yourself to a place of safety requires good judgment.

Making the decision to say "No" to drugs and other harmful substances can not only save your life but help determine the quality of your life.

Some of you may even have a driver's license and be charged with the legal responsibility of safely operating a two-ton vehicle that could not only kill you, but your passengers and the passengers of any vehicle you might strike.

In short, while you may be young, you do have the ability to be responsible for your safety. Toward that end, I would like you to make me a promise that you will NEVER work on a back handspring without the proper supervision of your parents, a cheer coach, or a gymnastics coach.

In addition, especially if you are a cheerleader, martial artist, or dancer, you may find that you are performing a back handspring or more advanced tumbling skills in unique circumstances and different tumbling surfaces.

For instance, a cheerleader typically performs tumbling passes while wearing some form of athletic shoe, which is a different experience than tumbling in bare feet. Dancers may perform acrobatic skills on a stage and martial artists may perform acrobatic skills on surfaces with less resilience than a normal tumbling mat.

Gymnasts may also do exhibitions in the park on panel mats which can become scorching hot under the sun or slippery when the dew begins to collect on them.

The point of all of the above is that you must consult with your coach who will help you adapt your techniques based on the conditions for performance to make sure you are safe.

Safety Oath

I promise to practice my gymnastics, acrobatic, or tumbling skills, including the back handspring, only when I am being properly supervised.

Athlete's Signature

Thank you! Now I can sleep better knowing you are safe. **Special Note:** If you find that, you are unable or unwilling to agree to this condition, then please gift another more responsible and desiring individual with this copy of the book.

Please email a note with the "Subject Line:" *I Always Focus on Safety!* to **coachrik@aol.com** and I will send you updates on techniques and ideas for improving your tumbling.

Glossary of Terms [31]

Amplitude: The amount of lift, repulsion, or extension of a particular skill. The explosive power demonstrated in gymnastics skills via height attained in the performance of a skill or range of motion of specific body parts.

Apparatus: A piece of equipment used in gymnastics training or competition.

Arabesque: A pose on one leg with the other leg extended behind the body.

Arch position: A curvature of the body in a reverse direction.

Attitude: The mental frame of reference displayed by a gymnast.

Back handspring: A move where a gymnast normally takes off from two feet, jumps backward through a handstand position onto the hands and snaps down to land on the feet; also known as a "flic-flac" or "flip-flop".

Back: 1) A backward somersault; 2) a direction of travel; and, 3) a part of the body.

Back Walkover: A gymnast starts in stretch position; lifts one leg to horizontal, and then reaches back with the upper body as one unit, using the flexibility in shoulders and back to reach down to the floor, and then pushes off support while pulling through the abdominal muscles to bring the lower body up and through the handstand position to finally step down and finish in an arabesque position.

Balance beam: A sixteen-foot beam, 4-inches wide and approximately 4-feet above the floor, used for routines involving leaps, turns and tumbling moves in women's artistic gymnastics.

Balance: A static position like a scale or handstand position.

Block Angle: Used to describe the position of the gymnast at takeoff leading into a skill.

Bridge: An arched position with the feet and hands flat on the floor, arms and legs straight, and the abdomen and hips clear of the floor.

Candlestick: A balance position high on the shoulders, with the hip angle open and body extended.

Cartwheel: A sideways / lateral kick to handstand then step down sideways with arms and legs extended.

Contraction: A forward movement of the torso, then a retraction of the abdominal wall.

Dismount: The ending or final skill performed in a routine.

---

[31] This glossary was created by combining terms from several sources: "Gymnastics: A Guide for Parents and Athletes," "Sequential Gymnastics II," Women's Junior Olympic Compulsory Exercises - 1997," and author's descriptions.

Element: A single skill or dance movement.

Execution: The form, style, amplitude, timing and technique used to complete a specific skill.

Extension: The movement of a body part to its full length or range of motion.

Flexibility: Flexibility is the range of motion through which a body part, such as the shoulders or legs, can move without feeling pain, while maintaining strength and stability of the joint.

Flexion / Flex: The tightening or shortening of a muscle or parts of the body into a more compact form.

Flic-flac / Flip-flop: A move where a gymnast takes off from one or two feet, jumps backward onto the hands and lands on the feet; also known as a "flip-flop" or "back handspring".

Flip: (generic term) Any rotation of the body, usually in the air, occurring in a forward or backward direction.

Floor exercise: An event in men's and women's artistic gymnastics where a gymnast performs a series of exercises on an open 42' by 42' square of mats (with springs, foam blocks, or a ski system underneath) covered with carpet.

Forward roll: A 360-degree revolution of the body forward (tuck, pike, straddle) in which the body is in contact with the floor or apparatus.

Front Handspring: from a step, run, or hurdle, the gymnast kicks up and through a handstand position, continuously driving her heels over and punching out of her shoulders to land standing in a stretch position.

Front Scale: By lifting one leg slightly above horizontal in the back, keeping the support leg straight, and keeping the head and chest (with arms extended to the sides or in line with the ears) just above horizontal the gymnast balances on one leg holding a front scale.

Front Walkover: A gymnast starts in stretch position; lifts one leg to horizontal, and then reaches through a "T" position to a handstand with her legs in a 180-degree split position. Using the flexibility in shoulders and lower-back she then transfers the weight from her shoulders and hands to her hips and legs. Pushing off the ground through shoulders and arms, she also pulls through her abdominal muscles to bring her upper body up and to a standing stretch position.

Handspring: (Front handspring) A common term for a gymnastics element where the gymnast kicks up to and through a handstand by punching out of the shoulders and driving the heels over to land in a stand. (Back handspring) From a stand the gymnast jumps backward to land in a handstand position from which he or she snaps down to a stand.

Handstand: Hands are flat on the floor, shoulder width apart, and the body completely extended and straight, with legs together, stomach sucked in, hips tucked under, and chest hollow.

Headstand: Place the hands and forehead on the floor in a triangular shape (head in front of hands), and extend the hips and legs straight upward over the triangular base of support.

Heel Drive: Occurs when a gymnast rapidly elevates both legs in a backward – upward direction.

Hop: Take off one foot to land on the same foot (two foot hops also).

Hurdle: The hurdle is a transition from a run or jump into a gymnastics skill.

Inverted: Any position in which the lower body is in a position above the upper body.

Jump: An explosive straightening of the legs that lifts the gymnast's body clear of the floor or apparatus.

Landing Mat: A four to eight-inch mat filled with foam and ethyfoam (generic term) to soften the landing when a gymnast dismounts the apparatus.

Layout: A straight or slightly arched position of the body. (may also be hollow)

Leap: Moving from one foot to the other foot showing flight.

Lunge: A lunge is a position in which one leg is flexed approximately 90 degrees, and the other leg is straight and extended. The body is stretched and upright over the flexed leg.

Mount: The skill used to begin a routine.

Neutral: Usually used to describe the position of the head, which is facing forward with no tilt forward or backward, and no turn either left or right.

Panel Mats: Basic mats which are constructed of a single layer of resilient foam, ranging in thickness from one to two inches, that can be folded into panels approximately two feet wide.

Pike: A position where the body is bent forward at the hips to 90 degrees or more while the legs are kept straight, with the thighs close to the upper body.

Pointed/Flexed Toes: A pointed toe is the proper position for achieving the maximum number of points in a gymnastics routine. A "Flexed" toe causes an unconscious, Pavlovian response in all coaches who will immediately yell, "Point your toes!"

Progressions: A series of skills trained in a specific order from basic to advanced.

Prone: Lying face down with the body straight.

Punch: Rebounding off the floor or apparatus. Jumping involves bending your legs and pushing, while "punching" involves anticipating the floor with tight legs and rebounding using the spring from the floor as well as power in your legs.

Rear: A descriptive term indicating that the body passes over or around an apparatus with the back of the body leading or facing the apparatus.

Rebound: A quick punch or bounce using very little flexion of the hips, knees, or ankles.

Repetition / Rep: The completion of one skill or motion in a prescribed series of motions. For example, a gymnast is told to complete 3 sets of 10 push-ups; doing one push-up would count as one repetition of the first set of 10 push-ups.

Rhythm: The speed or tempo at which a skill/dance step is performed.

Roll: Any 360-degree revolution of the body (forward, backward, sideways) in which the body is in contact with the floor or apparatus.

Round-off: A round-off is a dynamic turning movement. The gymnast steps forward and pushes off one leg while swinging-kicking the back leg upward in a fast cartwheel type motion. As the body becomes inverted, the legs come together and a 90-degree turn is executed; then pushing-punching off the hands-shoulders, the legs are snapped down to a landing facing the direction from which the performer started.

Rotation: Circular motion around an axis. A forward roll is a rotation, as is a twist.

Routine: A combination of gymnastic, acrobatic, and dance elements (depending on the apparatus) displaying a full range of skills and meeting the judging requirements of the particular level of competition.

Salto: a slang term (like "somi") for a somersault (in the air).

Set: 1) to perform a specific lead-up skill in preparation for a more advanced skill; 2) a slang term for the completion of one routine; 3) the completed repetitions of a conditioning exercise.

Setting: 1) The act of preparing or performing a specific lead-up move into a more advanced skill. 2) Preparing an apparatus by establishing height and width parameters appropriate to the athlete as well as preparing the workout and landing area with matting appropriate to the skills being performed.

Sequence: Two or more positions or skills, which are performed together creating a different skill or activity.

Side splits: A position where a gymnast sits on the floor with the legs at full horizontal extension on opposite sides of the body, forming a 180-degree split.

Skill: A particular gymnastics element or physical ability.

SLP: Safety Landing Position. When landing from a gymnastics skill the athlete lands with knees bent, lower back rounded, and arms up next to the ears.

Snap: A very quick movement of the body, usually from a 3/4 handstand position, where the gymnast quickly hollows her chest and drives her feet to the ground while lifting the torso to an upright position.

Split leap: A forward leap from one foot, landing on the opposite foot and assuming a split position in mid-air.

Splits: A position where one leg is extended forward and the other backward, at right angles to the body.

Spot: 1) To spot is to physically guide and/or assist a gymnast while performing a skill. Coaches spot for safety and when they are teaching new skills. 2) To spot can also mean to look for a specific point of orientation during the performance of a skill to have a reference point for the finish.

Spotters: Usually the coach or an individual whose job it is to protect competitors from injury should they fall.

Squared hips: A position of the body whereby both hips are flat and facing forward.

Squat: Support on the balls of the feet with the knees and hips flexed so that the seat is near, but not touching the floor with the heels and torso erect.

Stick: A gymnast "sticks" a landing when he/she executes a landing with correct technique and no movement of the feet and certainly no falls to the floor.

Straddle: A position in which the legs are straight and extended sideward.

Straddle split: The gymnast sits on the floor with her legs apart creating a 180-degree angle with her hips. From above, you should be able to draw a straight line (passing through her hips) from one foot to the other.

Stretch Position: Standing straight with the arms extended above your head.

Supine (Layout Position): Lying flat on the back with the body straight, arms extended above the head.

Tape (Gymnastics Tape): A specialized semi-porous tape that is 1 ½ "wide with a cloth and a sticky side used for making tape grips for bars, wrapping the wrists, taping ankles, and many other uses. See a sports trainer for specific guidelines on how to tape properly.

Timer: A set up drill that teaches the gymnast the proper sequence and timing for performing a skill.

T-Position: The "T" position looks exactly like a front scale, except the gymnast continues moving through the position to kick up to a handstand. Imagine from fingertips to toes, the gymnast's body is as tight as a teeter-totter board (from the playground); just as the board maintains a straight position going up and down on each end, the gymnast maintains a tight, stretched body position that resembles a "T" (with straight support leg) when going into and out of skills.

Tripod: Place the hands and forehead on the floor in a triangular shape (head in front of hands), and extend the hips above the triangular base. The body is piked with the knees bent, resting on the elbows.

Tuck: A position where the knees and hips are bent and drawn into the chest.
Turn: A rotation on the body's axis supported by one or both feet.

Twist: A move in acrobatic skills where a gymnast rotates around the body's longitudinal axis, defined by the spine.

V-sit: A position where the legs are raised off the floor close together and the body is supported by the hands to form a "V" shape.

Walkover: See **"Front Walkover,"** or **"Back Walkover."**

Wedge: A developmental mat filled with soft, shock absorbent foam. Its distinct shape is a sloping triangle with various heights and widths.

Wedgie: When an athlete's leotard or shorts ride up in the back.

* * * * * * * *

**Keep checking
www.GymnasticsTrainingTips.com
for new books and special reports.**

Coaches – Parents – Athletes:

Did you know that this book can be used as a **great fundraising item:**
- for your gym,
- parent's organization,
- for sale at invitational meets and cheer competitions,
- or for each athlete to raise money for meet / competition fees, uniforms / leotards / warm-ups, and travel expenses?

Check the **GymnasticsTrainingTips.com** web site for more information.

<u>Gymnastics Equipment</u>: Training at Home

As I have said more than once in this book, repetition, along with appropriate feedback and variety in the training system are the keys to success in training.

I have also noted that you should always focus on safety and since I know you will more than likely practice some of these skills at home, I am going to suggest, really demand, you get the appropriate safety equipment.

The basic equipment needed for practicing the skills listed in this book (after you have had initial training by a qualified coach):

1. Fold up tumbling mats. I suggest at least two tumbling mats. One to place under your landing cushion and one to extend beyond your typical landing area.
2. An 8" landing cushion. For practicing skills at home, this landing cushion will certainly soften the landings.
3. A foam barrel, that comes with a removable wedge, which makes the barrel look somewhat like a Pac man when the wedge is removed.
4. A wedge or incline mat – sometimes called the cheese (not illustrated).

For more information on home training equipment, contact:

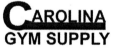 **AROLINA**
GYM SUPPLY
575 Dimmocks Mill Road
Hillsborough, NC 27278

www.carolinagym.com
info@carolinagym.com

877-496-7883 – Toll free.
919-732-1510 – Fax

About the Author

Several pizza's and many years ago, Rik Feeney was a competitive gymnast through High School and Temple University. During his career, Rik owned and worked at private gymnastics clubs where he trained gymnasts from state to national level competitors.

Rik is the author of several books on the sport of gymnastics, the first of which was *"Gymnastics: A Guide for Parents and Athletes"* – available via email at **www.GymnasticsTrainingTips.com**.

He has gone on to ghostwrite and continue authoring his own books with a new series titled "Gymnastics Education Modules" or **GEM's ™** which includes techniques for popular gymnastics and tumbling skills as well as information for parents and spectators.

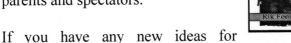

If you have any new ideas for techniques you would like to add to this document or have comments for the author, you can send them care of **coachrik@aol.com** .

Richardson Publishing is looking for material from new authors. If you have an idea or specialized knowledge you believe would make a good book or booklet, send a query letter care of the address listed on the back cover.

Printed in the United States
77927LV00003B/356